DISCARD

D1550652

To

_____

From

_____

Date

_____

# A WOMAN'S DAILY WALK WITH GOD

## ELIZABETH GEORGE

HARVEST HOUSE PUBLISHERS
EUGENE, OREGON

*Cover by Dugan Design Group, Bloomington, Minnesota*

*Cover photo © iStockphoto / 101cats / Vetta Collection*

**A WOMAN'S DAILY WALK WITH GOD**
Copyright © 2012 by Elizabeth George

Published by Harvest House Publishers
Eugene, Oregon 97402
www.harvesthousepublishers.com

ISBN 978-0-7369-4495-3 (pbk.)
ISBN 978-0-7369-4496-0 (eBook)

**Printed in China**

12 13 14 15 16 17 18 19 20 / FC-KBD / 10 9 8 7 6 5 4 3 2 1

*Dear Friend,*

As I often say at my conferences, "A lot of things can happen to a child of God in one day." So how are your days going? Most women tell me theirs are filled with surprises, speed bumps, road-blocks, and detours. I know this scenario all too well! Even a well-planned schedule for your hours can get totally derailed. Others tell me their days are filled with solitude and loneliness...or no adult company for mom. Truly, we never know what a day holds.

That's why a power-packed little book like this one can help you make it through your day and your dailies. Each devotion gives you a thrilling look at a truth from God. These meditations and reminders make it possible for you to carry a fresh, personal message from God into your sunrise. They arm you with thoughts and ideas for managing your heart when your plans go haywire. And they provide a special prayer to warm your soul and remind you of God's love and care—for you!

Begin now, and enjoy your daily journey into God's Word...and have a *great* day!

From my heart to yours,

Elizabeth George

# 1
# A Woman of Faith

*~·~*

*H*ow can you become a woman of faith? This pursuit can seem like a vague or difficult challenge sometimes. Take comfort. God's Word has a few things to say about this life-changing desire. How do you become a woman of faith who walks with God daily? Ephesians 2:8 says that faith comes by God's grace, and by grace we are saved. Faith is a work of God in your heart. And it's nurtured when you read the Bible.

When you are immersed in God's Word, you receive a close-up view of the trials, tests, and temptations others faced—and how they handled their situations with faith. You'll also discover how sometimes they failed. Romans 10:17 reminds us that "faith comes by hearing, and hearing by the word of God." When the Bible is taught, listen closely. Then be faithful in sharing the gospel—the faith you so richly enjoy.

*God, I want to be a woman of great faith. I look forward to nurturing my faith by reading Your Word and gathering its guidance, examples, and encouragement. I pray that I'll walk in Your truths through all of my days.*

# The Gift of a Day

~·~

*H*ave you opened the gift of today? It is right in front of you. You may have stepped over it on the way to building a career. You may have stepped around it while chasing a toddler. Or maybe you looked past it as you focused on future worries. My friend, today is the future. How you manage today for God adds to the quality of the life *and* the future you're building. The gift of a whole, precious, and priceless day shouldn't be wasted. Ask God, "Lord, how do You want me to live this day? What is it You want me to do with this one day that You've given me?" It puts everything in a different perspective, doesn't it?

> *God, this day is Your day. How should I spend it? I want to delight in the precious gift of living in Your purpose. I'm excited to interact with my family, engage in work, and explore the wonders of this day with Your perspective guiding me.*

# 3
# A Heart of Goodness

*D*o you know what's at the heart of a godly
woman? It's a heart of goodness that gives to
others. As a woman, you know all about giving.
You give as a woman, as a wife, as a mother. And
that's exactly what God planned. You're meant to
give and to do good and to operate out of a good
heart. The goodness you receive from God is a treasure for you to share with others. Don't hold back
when you have the chance to be gracious and generous. All you have is today. So this is the day that
counts for pursuing goodness and for dispensing it
to others. Make this little poem your prayer: "This
is the wish I always wish, the prayer I always pray;
Lord, may my life help other lives it touches by the
way."

> *God of goodness, let Your love and kindness flow
> through me. Guide my words and my first impulses
> so that I am quick to offer help, encouragement,
> and Your wisdom to the people in my life. Show me
> the needs and hurts of others so I can share Your
> endless goodness in personal ways.*

# Your First Love

~•~

*W*ouldn't it be nice to return to the passion and love you felt for God when you first believed? Take heart. I believe that you can "go back" to the spark of excitement and commitment you felt then. You can return to the first, powerful love you had for God.

Take a look at your faith life today. What is missing now that was a part of the days when you hungered for God? Do you need to return to church? To pick up your Bible and begin again to read God's precious Word? To kneel in prayer and nurture your prayer life all over again? To ask forgiveness from someone or from God? And what sin or obstacle do you need to let go of? Sometimes the first step forward is actually a step backward. Hosea 6:1 says: "Come, let us return to the LORD...he will heal us...he will bind up our wounds" (NIV). Return to the joy of your first love.

*Heavenly Father, I am so grateful for the day I first knew Your love and experienced Your grace. Help me return to the ways of devotion and obedience. Restore to me the joy of my salvation, dear Lord.*

# Your Full Potential

~•~

*W*hen was the last time you thought about your potential? Don't give up on the hope of God's plans for you. An ordinary person used *by* God is one who can do extraordinary things *for* God. Explore the story of Gideon in Judges 6. The Lord sent him to help save Israel. But Gideon said, "How can I save Israel? I'm the least in my family." And God said, "Gideon, I will be with you!" God saw something special in Gideon—something Gideon wasn't even aware of: potential. God took a fearful coward and transformed him into what is described in the Bible as a "mighty man of valor" (verse 12).

When God calls you to do or to become something beyond your ability, it is because He wants you to rely on His strength and power. What seemingly impossible task is God asking of you so that you may live out your full potential?

*Lord, thank You for planting seeds of hope in me. When I am discouraged or fearful, I need only to remember that I can be used by You to do something extraordinary.*

# *An Energized Life*

〜・〜

*A* woman shared her frustration: "I used to pray and read my Bible regularly. But now? I just don't have the interest I once did." Can you relate?

Life is busy and complicated. Where can you find the energy to add one more commitment? The truth is that God expects us to grow spiritually—for a reason you might not have considered. One of the best results of spiritual growth is energy—tremendous energy. As you read the Bible, the power of the Word of God recharges every activity you do. It brings God's perspective on your life and on your work. Everything you do receives that divine infusion of stamina, drive, purpose, enthusiasm. After all, you were created by God, and for God. Adding spiritual growth to your life means adding His life back into your day.

> *Lord, refresh my weary spirit. Forgive me for letting my spiritual growth take second, third, fourth place in my life. I want to be fueled by a thriving faith and empowered by Your strength and vitality.*

# A Noble Woman

~·~

$M$y prayer for you is that you will aspire to become a noble woman. A virtuous woman. Regardless of your background or how you were raised, this life is about you living out your great purpose as a godly woman. And in the Bible, God has preserved His portrait of what such a woman looks like through the Proverbs 31 woman. She models for us the traits that God so highly esteems and exalts. Take time to read through Proverbs 31 so you can admire, inspect, and study this woman's attitude, behavior, and faith. Hers was a heart of excellence. I pray that you will desire to pursue her level of commitment to family, others, and God. As Proverbs 31:29 says of her, "Many daughters have done well, but you excel them all." Let this be your legacy as a noble woman of God.

*God, shape my desires to be those of this special woman of virtue in Proverbs. In Your strength, I can adopt her qualities of excellence. I want to be a woman who lives out her days with faithfulness that brings You praise.*

# Caring, Creative, Confident

~·~

*C*aring. *Creative. Confident.* These three words definitely describe a woman who is walking with the Lord. You can discover the value of these traits in God's eyes when you visit the woman described in Proverbs 31:10-31. She worked industriously, and her creative abilities blossomed. Her skills grew until the end product of her efforts was excellent. As you place your confidence in the Lord—as you labor out of a full and joyful heart, work hard, and grow in the areas of your gifts, abilities, and skills—you'll discover the treasure of doing things well. Of benefiting others. And of spending precious time and energy in rewarding ways. What joy!

The close of Proverbs 31 offers encouragement: "A woman who fears the LORD, she shall be praised. Give her of the fruit of her hands, and let her own works praise her in the gates."

*God, may the work of my hands and the intentions of my heart result in creations, actions, and treasures that are pleasing to You and of use to those in my life. I pray to be a woman who labors and loves with a joyful heart.*

# 9
# God Will Provide

~•~

*I*'d feel so much better if I knew the plan—if I knew exactly what God had in mind for my life."

How well do you manage when it comes to trusting God? Do you trust Him to take care of your need for food and clothing? Or do you live in fear that perhaps He won't? Do you trust God to supply instruction, encouragement, protection, love, and friendship? Or do you fret about some perceived inability on God's part to care for you? Psalm 23:1 begins with "The LORD is my shepherd; I shall not want." When God oversees your days and nights, you will not be in need of anything. If you're single, God will provide. If you're childless, God will provide. If you're a widow, God will provide. Trust in Him. Relax in Him, and enjoy the sweet rest that faith provides.

*Lord, when I'm scared, tired, worried, or feeling aimless, I know that You care about me and every aspect of my life. You keep watch over Your flock night and day. You are my shepherd. I will never be in need.*

# 10
# Words Fitly Spoken

~•~

*W*hile communicating frequently and with many people seems to be the goals in the culture today, there is a much more godly goal for you to keep in mind. Proverbs 25:11 says, "A word fitly spoken is like apples of gold in settings of silver." This should be the hope and plan for *all* your communication, especially with the person most important to you—your husband. Here are just a few of God's keys to loving communication. Your words are to be soft. A soft answer turns away wrath, and a harsh word stirs up anger. The Bible says pleasant words promote understanding. Your words are to be suitable—sweet to the soul and health to the bones. And a difficult one for sure is "Everyone should be quick to listen, slow to speak and slow to become angry" (James 1:19 NIV). Let your words, expressions, and even your physical language be God's language.

*God, give me the right and righteous words to speak to my husband and others. Hold me back from careless and unhelpful comments. Let my words shine with the value of being well-chosen and kind.*

# Love Your Neighbors

~•~

Have you noticed how few people know their neighbors these days? It might seem convenient to not be overly involved with other people around you, but Jesus calls us to a deeper relationship. "'You shall love the Lord your God with all your heart, with all your soul, with all your strength, and with all your mind,' and 'your neighbor as yourself'" (Luke 10:27).

Love your neighbor as yourself. You were home free—*almost*—until that last little phrase. Prayer is how such a heart and such a love are cultivated. Pick one day each week to pray for your neighbors. Over time, you'll discover that these people have a sincere place in your heart and in your life. When you wave to them in passing, your heart will have a greater compassion and empathy for them. Through your prayers, God turns strangers into loved ones. It's one of the privileges of being faithful in all that you do.

*Lord, I do love You with all my heart and soul. Expand my circle of people to pray for and give me a sincere heart for my neighbors. Let compassion and kindness give me a tenderness toward their needs. Lord, help me be a true neighbor and friend to these people You've placed near me.*

# All About Attitude

Your attitude toward others, work, and your daily life is a reflection of your attitude toward God. God asks you to do your work with enthusiasm. He asks that you serve your employers and your family wholeheartedly, that you treat those you interact with throughout the day with respect. Ask God for a grateful, obedient heart. Your faithfulness, or lack of it, to God's direction is noticed by others. Are people getting an accurate picture of Jesus from your life?

Second Corinthians 3:2 reminds us that by our very lives—we are a living Bible, known and read by all. "You are our epistle written in our hearts, known and read by all men; clearly you are an epistle of Christ, ministered by us, written not with ink but by the Spirit of the living God, not on tablets of stone but on tablets of flesh, that is, of the heart."

So, what's the gospel according to *you*?

*Lord, help me to embrace an attitude that reflects the gospel of Your love. Reveal to me any ways that I can send a brighter message of Your hope through my actions, words, and decisions.*

# 13
# Above Average

~·~

There is a time for every woman when she can feel invisible. Have you had days when it seemed like nobody could see you? As if you blended right into the background? I think we all feel that way at some time or other. When you turn to God's view of you, you'll discover that you are anything but average or invisible. A woman who seeks God as her life-travelling companion stands out in many ways. Here are a few examples of what I mean: A godly woman is beyond average because she keeps her word. She honors her vows. She exhibits great faith. She overcomes great obstacles. And she affects her family, her community, even the world. Now it's your turn. Make a list of those qualities and godly traits you want in your life. Make it your prayer list. Be that woman after God's own heart.

*God, I'm excited about the ways You give my life value, light, and power. When I feel like I'm invisible, I will stand in the truth that You see and know me completely. I'm grateful for Your unfailing, all-knowing love.*

# Modeling Character

~•~

*D*o images of women presented in magazine photos, intriguing novels, and the movies have you wanting to become them? If you're looking for qualities that make you a godly woman, the examples on glossy covers and TV shows most likely don't come close. But don't give up. In God's Word there is a list of qualities that He desires for you to cultivate. Titus 2:4-5 encourages older women to teach the younger women to be loving, self-controlled, and pure; to do good, to be kind, to submit to their husbands. Embrace this biblical example of a godly woman, and then model that character to younger women. When your life becomes a living example of godly character, you will glorify God and honor His Word.

*Lord, I want to become a woman who honors and reflects Your character through my actions and behavior. Protect me from turning to the world's example so that I am able to walk the way of a godly woman.*

# The Testing of Your Faith

~·~

*L*oss and difficulty are a part of life. As a woman of faith, however, you can grow through the hardest of times. Here's an assignment: Jot down how old you'll be in ten years. Now write down what will probably happen in your life between now and then. A decade ago, I remember noting I'd probably lose both of my parents—and my husband's parents. Some of the changes I experienced were on my list. Some I never even dreamed of.

As God teaches you how to handle the tests of your faith, take heart in the wisdom found in James 1:2-4: "My brethren, count it all joy when you fall into various trials, knowing that the testing of your faith produces patience. But let patience have its perfect work, that you may be perfect and complete, lacking nothing." With God's help, your trial today is leading to your wholeness tomorrow.

*Lord, I cling to Your truths and promises as I experience change, sorrow, and good-byes. It gives me comfort to know that loss, through a spirit of perseverance, becomes a part of the fullness of Your will.*

# Who's to Blame?

_~•_~

*S*hifting blame seems to have replaced accepting responsibility. Isn't it amazing how many excuses you can come up with when you give in to temptation and blow it? And it's equally amazing how blame rises to the top of excuse-making methods. "It's her fault." "I couldn't help it." "Everybody's doing it." "Nobody's perfect." And of course the old standby—"I didn't know it was wrong."

If we're not to place responsibility on someone else for our circumstance, then who does that leave to blame? James 1:14 says, "Each one is tempted when he is drawn away by his own desires and enticed." James is saying to you to be aware of your *own* sin. Now that's not fun to hear—not at all. But it is wonderful to hear that you will more fully experience God's grace when you acknowledge the times you stumble and fall and go to Him for forgiveness.

> *Lord, give me the humility and the courage to accept responsibility for my own moments of temptation and sin. Show me the way to a vulnerable, honorable heart. I want to be pure before You through Your amazing grace.*

# A True Friend

⌒⸱⌒

*I*t's hard to find a true friend like the one described in Proverbs 18:24, who sticks closer than a brother or sister. It's also a challenge to be a good friend. How do you measure up? When others think of you, do they think of someone they can trust with their hopes and their troubles? Are you someone they can go to for wise counsel?

When you walk in the ways of God, your faithfulness is evident not just to friends but to your family too. Proverbs 31:11 celebrates that "the heart of her husband safely trusts" the virtuous woman. And how about your children? Do you keep your word to them? What can you do today to cultivate and nurture your character so that you can be this friend, this woman of honorable character?

*God, give me the strength and conviction to be a good friend and a faithful, wise wife and mom. I want to be a woman of virtue who brings You praise.*

# Chosen and Special

~·~

*A*n abused child will often describe herself as small, worth little more than an insect. And when she grows up to be a woman, her self-image has already taken a huge blow. My dear friend, if that describes you today, take time to embrace your identity in Christ. You are loved and held by the Lord.

The Bible says you're "chosen"—you're one of God's special people. Who you are in Christ is far more important and meaningful than whatever has taken place in your past. And as a child of God— one who has been purchased with the precious blood of Christ—you have incredible worth. God has done all this so that you may enjoy redemption, so that you may live in the excellency and quality of God Himself.

*Jesus, I give my past and my future to You because You make all things new. In You, I am special and whole. I have value as Your child. Nothing and no one can take that from me.*

# 19
# God Is in Control

*W*ho's in charge of your life? It's a great question. And if you desire to be a woman of God, it's one you need to be asking. Who *is* in charge, and who is leading the way in your life? God is. And because He's in control, you can face each day with His power and love. If you get tossed around today and some hard knocks come your way, turn them over to God. If you're struggling with a decision, bring it before God. If you've been hurt by others, admit your pain and trust God fully. And never seek revenge—no matter what. That impulse comes when we think others are in control. Psalm 147:5 declares, "Great is our Lord, and mighty in power; His understanding is infinite." God is in control!

*God, I trust that You are in control. I'm so grateful that I can give every situation, need, trouble, and hope to You. When I'm tempted to take charge, help me release my hold on things so that I can live in Your power and will.*

# Desire God's Wisdom

*I* don't know about you, but it seems like I have to make at least one decision a second. Some days, life just bombards us on all fronts, doesn't it? So, how do we get the kind of wisdom we need? In 1 Kings 3:9, Solomon prayed, "Give to Your servant an understanding heart to judge Your people, that I may discern between good and evil." Then, because Solomon asked for the right thing, God said, "I have given you a wise and understanding heart, so that there has not been anyone like you before you, nor shall any like you arise after you." And there was a bonus. God not only gave to Solomon what he asked, but also gave riches and honor among all the kings of his day. Desire God's wisdom—above *all* else.

*God, I get overwhelmed by the many decisions and demands of life. Give me an understanding heart and lead me through my days with Your wisdom.*

# 21
# Check Your Prayers

~·~

"W hat do I pray for? That's easy. My husband and children and that we can pay the bills this month!"

What do you lift up to God in your quiet time? Be sure it's that *one* thing that will help *every*thing in your life. One of my favorite verses is Proverbs 2:3. It says, "Cry out for discernment, and lift up your voice for understanding." That covers a lot of ground. It takes some sweat and a few tears to pursue God's wisdom. How strenuously are you seeking understanding? Do you seek it as though you are searching for hidden treasure, with a heart of passion, anticipation, and hopefulness? Are you searching the Scriptures? I leave you with this encouragement from James 1:5: "If any of you lacks wisdom, you should ask God, who gives generously to all without finding fault, and it will be given to you" (NIV). Now that's a promise you can take to heart.

*Lord, I need discernment. Help me to understand the riches of Your Word. I want to pursue the treasures of Your promises so that my prayers, decisions, and dreams come from a right understanding of Your will and Your way.*

# Stop the Frustration

~•~

Does your day start off like a race against time as you maneuver through a long to-do list and unexpected obstacles? If you're rushing in all directions at once, *stop*. Breathe. When your priorities are out of whack, you end up going through your days with guilt and frustration, and rarely with a sense of accomplishment and purpose. But the wise woman puts God first. Include one very practical decision in your schedule every day: Read something out of God's Word. After all, He's the source of the wisdom you're looking for. And He's revealed it in His Word—the Bible. Before the day gets out of hand, curl up in some cozy place and read your Bible. Fill your mind with God's mind. Beginning each day with God will change your priorities.

*Father, fill my heart with the desires of Your heart. I will set my eyes on the priorities that You give to me. I'm tired of rushing around without the peace and assurance of Your wisdom. Show me the way, Lord, and I will walk in it.*

# God in Your Plans

〜•〜

*I*t's Thursday. I need to call Mom, pick up Dave's dry cleaning, take Melinda to the dentist, stop by the bank, then go to that parent-teacher conference at 4:00." If this list reminds you of your own schedule, take out your planner and see what's slated for tomorrow. Have you included any time with God? Put God in your planner—as the *first* thing. When I do this simple act, I never fail to hear Jesus' words in my heart: "Elizabeth, without Me you can do nothing."

Get up 30 minutes earlier tomorrow. Begin your day with God, and you'll start discovering a rich reward. Oh, you'll be tired. Count on it. But you'll also discover fulfillment and refreshment because you are walking with God. Live your days according to God's top two priorities: God first, others second. It's an incredible formula to draw you closer to God's heart.

*God, I will put You first in my day and in all that I do. I long for Your presence. Help me to be obedient and faithful so that I can walk in and experience Your transforming love and priorities.*

# One Day at a Time

〜•〜

You want to be healthy and fit. And, if you're like most women, you have some weeks of good effort, and some of more weakness than success. This pattern can lead some women to lose and gain the same 20 pounds over and over. But this day forward can be different. Just keep telling yourself, "One day at a time."

Here are a handful of God's timeless principles right out of His Word to shed light on your desire to shed pounds or bad habits. Proverbs 23:2 says, "Control yourself if you have a big appetite" (NCV). As much as that hurts to hear and as hard as it is to do, it's God's way toward real change. First Corinthians 11:28 reminds us to examine ourselves for sinful habits. Galatians 5:22-23 shines a light on the fruit of the Spirit, including self-control. Remember, one day at a time. But let the conviction from God's Word affect your decisions right now. Then extend these healthier habits for a lifetime.

*Lord, it is so difficult to let go of unhealthy habits. Help me lean into Your strength so I can commit to healthy changes even as I face the temptations and challenges of the day.*

# Character and Strength

$\sim\cdot\sim$

*I* remember the day I discovered the meaning
of the word *virtuous*. It was one of those red-
letter days that became a turning point in my growth
as a Christian woman. I was reading the Bible and
God gave me a simmering desire for the character
and strength of the woman I was reading about in
Proverbs 31. Have you read that chapter? I decided
to pursue her excellence and commitment. I began
to apply my energy to better things than nonstop
reading and excessive TV viewing. I wanted to be
strong in character. I longed to be powerful in mind
and in body.

The Proverbs 31 woman inspired me to become
more efficient and to use my abilities for God's purposes. Meeting this woman in the pages of my Bible
helped me discover how and what to strive for in
my daily walk. Let the Proverbs 31 woman speak to
your life and provide you with a beautiful illustra-
tion of virtue and excellence.

*Lord, thank You for the power and vision of what
it means to be a woman of godly character. Let
her example become a source of inspiration for my
spiritual growth.*

# Pursue Good Works

~•~

*I*s there anything better than knowing your life overflows with good and godly works? What wasted time and energy—and lives—when you and I live for ourselves. First Timothy 5:9-10 gives you a checklist of the traits for a good reputation, including bringing up children, lodging strangers, washing the saints' feet, relieving the afflicted, and diligently following every good work.

Whether married, single, widowed, young, or old, you earn your good reputation by living above reproach and doing good. You can use your home to welcome and encourage others. Commit your time to assisting people who're hurting. Visit the sick. Pray for the needs of others. Help a busy mom out with her kids. Befriend and mentor a younger woman. Devote your time, energy, and heart diligently—in a life of good works!

*Heavenly Father, let my good works bring glory to Your name. When my efforts of care and kindness build a solid reputation, may I always be quick to give You praise and honor. Good works reflect the great love You bestow on me.*

# Prayer—God's Way

*A*re your prayers becoming a bit lopsided? Do you pray for troubles to follow someone else or for things to go your way only? There's definitely a right *and* a wrong way to pray. And often the wrong way is when you ask things for the wrong reasons.

Be sure to lift your motives before the Lord. Ask Him to take a look at your heart when you bring your requests to Him. And be willing to acknowledge your sinful motives and adjust them. Your motives have got to match up with God's will, with what He tells you in His Word is pleasing to Him.

Prayer is an incredible gift from God. Pursue prayer and reap the blessings of "a gentle and quiet spirit" (1 Peter 3:4).

*Heavenly Father, search my heart and its motives when I pray. Draw me near to You so that I can listen for Your discernment and pray only with godly purposes. Today I pray specifically that my thoughts, heart, and prayers be pure and pleasing in Your sight.*

# Lots of Bible

~•~

*W*hat would the condition of your Bible tell me about your spiritual life? Does a worn cover reveal daily use? Have past tears left traces of your pain and joy on the thin pages? Or is your Bible tucked away on a shelf and covered in dust?

There was a time when I dusted off an old Bible—to save my marriage. My marriage was going from bad to worse and I chose to read the only religious book I could find in our home—a Bible. Lots of Bible. Before I'd finished reading, I gave my life and my relationship with my husband to Christ. Over the years, I went through what I call the three stages of Bible reading: The cod liver oil stage, when it's like medicine; the shredded wheat stage, when it's nourishing but dry. And finally the peaches-and-cream stage, when it's consumed with passion and pleasure. Dust off that Bible. It has the answers you're looking for, and its delights await you.

*God, I have a renewed hunger for Your truth, wisdom, and love. I am ready to experience the transforming power of Your Word each day. May I reach for the Bible and receive it as my lifeline.*

# Read the Manual

~·~

*W*hen you can't fit the pieces of life together, have you ever cried out, "I need an instruction manual!" You are entirely correct. You do need an instruction manual. But what you may have forgotten is that you have already been given one—the Bible. God's Word is written for and to you, but it won't help you put order and meaning into your life unless you read it. The only wrong way to read the Bible is to *not* read it.

I have a secret to share with you. Don't make your Bible reading time an ordeal. Make it the treat that it is. Get a cup of coffee or tea or hot chocolate. Sit down, open God's Word, and read. Take it with you to the doctor's office, the beach, or on an airplane. Then "sip away" on God's Word any place you are.

*Lord, take this mess of my life. I want to exchange it for Your purpose and plan for me. You bring order, beauty, meaning, and significance to my journey when I follow Your instruction. Lead me, Lord. I will follow.*

# The Perfect Listener

~•~

*I*'ve heard from many women that they would pray more often, but they aren't sure what to say or they worry they are saying the wrong things. Don't ever worry about what you will say to God. He's heard it all. Have you ever had a young child try to communicate with you? You appreciate the effort, don't you? If your heart is right, there is no such thing as a badly done prayer.

That young child I mentioned? You eagerly listen through the fidgeting and jabbering as they search for words in their limited vocabulary. You hang on every sound because you don't want to miss a thing. And you receive great delight in their willingness and enthusiasm to express their hearts. Your heavenly Father hears your prayers with the same delight and with even greater grace and joy because He is perfect. Perfectly kind. Perfectly patient. He loves it when you and I come to Him with our prayers.

*Father, I will speak from my heart to Your heart without worries. I'm so grateful that I can come to You with my questions, worries, praises, and hopes, and You listen with the attention of a loving Father. Thank You.*

# 31
# God Is Faithful

~·~

Faithfulness is a necessary part of a healthy relationship. A faithful person can be trusted in what they do and what they say. Are you that person for friends and family members? Do you have the blessing of such people in your life?

No matter what your situation, God is the one you can always go to with the assurance of being safe, heard, and cared for.

And there is more wonderful news—God is always faithful, even when you sin. The Bible says if you are faithful to confess your sin, He is faithful and just to forgive you your sins and to cleanse you from all unrighteousness.

God is unchanging and unchangeable. Draw close to Him with your every need, and experience the peace of His faithfulness.

*God, Your presence is my refuge. When I call out to You, I know that You are listening. I confess my sins and my weaknesses to You and Your love for me remains strong, unchanged. This true love shows me the way of faithfulness.*

# What Is Sin?

*T*he world can make the concept of sin quite blurry. So, what *is* it exactly? Well, the Bible has the answer, so stay with me. Sin is any thought, word, or action that goes against God's standards. So if we're going to grow spiritually as God intends, sin has to be dealt with. First Peter 2:1-3 gives us a clear view of what sin is and why we need to bring it to God: "Therefore, laying aside all malice, all deceit, hypocrisy, envy, and all evil speaking, as newborn babes, desire the pure milk of the word, that you may grow thereby, if indeed you have tasted that the Lord is gracious."

What you say and do matters. Reflect on the patterns of your life. Are any warning lights flashing? Acknowledge all sins to God, including those "little white lies" that keep you from the spiritual growth God desires for you. As a woman of God, you will exchange the bitterness of sin for the taste of the Lord's grace.

*Forgive me, Lord. I have sinned in small and big ways. I've let jealousy and pride direct my actions. I desire the pure milk of Your Word. It nourishes me and shows me how to live a godly life. Lord, Your grace is so sweet, it inspires me to grow strong in Your ways.*

# The Best Choice

*I* should get up, but I'd rather pull the covers over my head and go back to sleep this morning!" Well, that's one way to handle the first decision of the day, but not the *best* way. It's like the "E" word: *exercising*. I can either do it or let it slide for another 24 hours. And then another. But let's call the reason for these decisions what it is—laziness.

A far more serious choice than sleeping in or skipping a workout is the choice to not exercise your spiritual growth in God's Word. Growth requires strength and nourishment that comes from God's living, powerful, life-changing promises. Honor God and make a renewed commitment to make better choices. In fact, I urge you to make the very best choice—spend more quiet time before the Lord and immersed in His Word.

*God, when I neglect to exercise my faith, I notice the consequences. My prayer life becomes weak. I feed on the junk food of worldly distractions. And temptations seem mightier than my self-control. Help me make the best choice—the choice for You and Your Word.*

# 34
# Sharing the Journey

*I*t isn't easy to be a godly woman. It takes commitment and desire to pursue spiritual growth and a closer relationship with the Lord. But here's encouragement for your pursuit of a deeper faith: Look for another woman who has the maturity, biblical wisdom, and experience you need, and ask for her help.

If you're the mature woman in the Lord, take a younger woman under your wing. Encourage her in the Lord. As a new believer, I knew I didn't know anything. So I went looking for someone who knew more than I. I'm eternally grateful to those women who patiently worked with me—and gently encouraged my spiritual growth. Some pushed. Some pulled. And some carried me part of the way. I'm a debtor to those loving saints! A shared journey of faith is a rich, abundant one.

*God, help me find a mentor who can model maturity in faith and obedience. Then lead me to a young woman who needs my encouragement, honesty, and prayerfulness. It is such a gift to share my daily walk with others.*

# A Generous Soul

*I*t's natural to enjoy the comforts and benefits of money. But there's a lot more to consider if you desire to be rich in spirit. The Bible warns against the love of money: "The love of money is a root of all kinds of evil, for which some have strayed from the faith in their greediness" (1 Timothy 6:10). The best way to guard against loving money is to be generous. Proverbs 11:25 calls you to be a "generous soul." Who needs your money today? What missionary's ministry could be bettered by a gift from you? What child in poverty could be sponsored? How could your church benefit from your generosity?

Take your advice from 2 Corinthians 8:7: "Since you excel in everything—in faith, in speech, in knowledge, in complete earnestness and in the love we have kindled in you—see that you also excel in this grace of giving" (NIV). Find ways to become an excellent giver—a generous soul.

*God, release me from my desire for money and material riches. I want my longings to be for the wealth of Your wisdom and generosity so that I will give freely of my possessions and become a loving steward of all my blessings.*

# A Dream Come True

*T*ime for me? You're kidding, right? I'm wife, mom, and driver 24/7/365!" Has the idea of taking a moment or two for yourself become the impossible dream? Well, be encouraged, my weary friend. *Some* dreams come true.

Your life's a bit like a battery. It needs to be recharged on a regular basis. When you plan some time for yourself to grow spiritually, to develop your spiritual gifts, to refine your talents, and to grow as a person, you're preparing yourself for a ministry to others—starting with your busy and hectic family. If you want to have an influence on others, plan time for yourself. And walk with God each step of the way. Second Peter 3:18 puts it this way: "Grow in the grace and knowledge of our Lord and Savior Jesus Christ."

Time for you? You bet. A lot depends on how well you grow your spiritual life.

*Lord, give me peace about taking some time for me and my personal spiritual growth. Reveal to me ways that I can make room for this priority. I long to rest in Your grace and knowledge and to become the woman You created me to be.*

# Be Bold

~·~

God is definitely a gift-giving God. And one of the gifts He gave me was a special friend with a passion for flower arranging. Her dramatic pieces took on a life of their own under the direction of her hands. I asked Julie why her arrangements were so extraordinary. What made them so spectacular? With just two words, Julie changed my life. She said, "Be bold!" It's her motto for everything she does. *Be* bold. And *live* boldly for God. Think about what your life will look like if you follow this motto.

What you do today is important because you're exchanging a day of your life for it. So what do you want the next 24 hours to be about? As you consider your answer, keep Julie's motto in mind. After all, He's given you life in Himself. He has purposes in mind for your life! Be bold? You bet!

*Father, this day is my gift from You. I surrender my plans so I can embrace Your wonderful design for my life. I look forward to living out my faith, hopes, love, and purpose with the beautiful freedom of boldness.*

# A Masterpiece

~•~

*A*re you operating in survival mode? Many women have given up using their organizers and other plan-making methods out of frustration. If you've thrown in the time-management towel, I want you to give it another try. Determine to make tomorrow a better day than yesterday. Ask God for His wisdom. Just for today, create a schedule, even if it's a "bad" one. Any schedule is better than no schedule. Scheduling is a necessity. It's a mirror of your life. A tool for improvement. And it's a "wand" for accomplishment.

Think about the creation of the world. God had a schedule—from before the foundation of the world. He knew exactly what He would create each day—that first and most glorious week of the history of all creation. It was a true masterpiece. And He knew He would rest on the seventh day. How about you? How's your masterpiece looking?

*God, I will commit to scheduling my time. I will follow Your lead and create a plan for this day, this week, and maybe even beyond. Show me what it means to be faithful to good intentions and godly priorities.*

# Fun Together

~·~

*I*f you're married, do you and your husband have fun together? Are you able to keep the kindness and love kindled? It grieves me to hear any woman say that her marriage has lost its joy. The time you spend with your husband is such a gift—one that can be taken away too early. So, make time for fun! My Jim and I work hard, but we also commit to spending time together for activities we enjoy as a couple. We regularly make room in our schedules for recreation, hobbies, and interests. A Saturday of kayaking or wandering through flea markets or bookstores is a treat. Fun for us is walking through the grand lobbies of hotels we could never afford to stay in. We sit and have coffee in the lush atmosphere. And as we sip and pretend, we have a great time of connection and laughter. Not bad for the price of two cups of coffee!

What's fun for you and your husband? Make time and make a plan. It is worth investing effort toward joy.

> *Lord, remind me of the simple ways my husband and I enjoy each other's company and shared experiences. Give us the gift of fun, delight, and memorable moments to boost our spirits and to strengthen our bond.*

# Small Things Matter

~•~

*I*t was such an insignificant sin. What's the big deal?" Have you caught yourself thinking this? It is tempting to overlook your sins when those around you are dismissive of smaller transgressions. It's just one TV program; one date with an unbeliever; one more small debt. But small things matter. When you say, "What's the harm?" consider whether you are choosing to be faithful or disobedient. Does your choice make you God's friend or the world's friend?

What kinds of choices have you made today, this week, this month? What's the pattern of those choices? James 4:4 strikes a warning you can't ignore. It says, "Do you not know that friendship with the world is enmity with God?" Turn your eyes on Jesus. Be consumed with God's Word, utterly absorbed in Him.

*Heavenly Father, I humbly seek to live for You. Grant me the grace to do that. Unveil those transgressions that I have allowed to be a part of my daily life. I desire an unwavering and uncompromised friendship with You.*

# God's Plan and Promise

~•~

*I*'ve got my whole life ahead of me." "There's still time to get to that." "Someday I will make my spiritual life a priority." The truth is there are no guarantees about what tomorrow will bring. That makes this moment and this day all the more important.

What is God's plan and purpose for you? In the end, what do you want to have accomplished with your life? What do you want to leave behind? Life will have its obstacles—no question. But you can look forward to an eternal life with God. Psalm 16:11 promises, "You will show me the path of life; in Your presence is fullness of joy; at Your right hand are pleasures forevermore."

Do you have that hope today? It's a gift of God given to you through faith in God's Son, Jesus Christ. You can live each day, no matter what, in the confidence of God's promise.

*Father in heaven, I am ready to walk in Your purpose and to give my days eternal meaning. I embrace Your promises and the amazing gift of eternal life through Your Son, Jesus Christ.*

# Life Management

~•~

*W*here has the time gone? The day is over, or maybe the week is over, and all your good intentions have simply vanished. What happened? Time management experts say they often hear the words, "I wish I knew how to manage my time better." But rarely do they hear, "I wish I knew how to manage *myself* better." As you seek God's wisdom regarding your time, the question to ask is, "How could I manage my life better in order to use the little time I do have?"

The priorities you set are life-determining. Life doesn't just happen to you. Your choices and decisions are a reflection of how well you've set and followed your priorities. Your life—with its minutes, hours, days, and years—is brimming with possibilities. With God's help, you can manage your life one day at a time.

> *Jesus, I need to manage myself better. You've seen me struggle with a lack of energy and focus. I will look to the foundation of Your Word to shape my priorities and my heart. I want a life that demonstrates Your plans and possibilities for me fulfilled.*

# Choose Your Words

W hen unkind words are spoken about you or behind your back, they might trigger an impulse to respond with negative remarks. But you have a choice about the kind of words you speak. If you desire to walk closely with the Lord today, you will make the choice to keep your words and your thoughts clear of spite, falseness, or anger. Gossip is definitely not an option. Proverbs 25:11 sets the standard: "A word fitly spoken is like apples of gold in settings of silver." You can speak, or not speak. You can destroy or build with your words. You can spread hatred or love. You can discourage or encourage. Scream or speak softly. Begin by making the choice to *not* speak evil of one another. We're to be peaceable and considerate and show true humility toward all. A *loving* word heals and blesses. Consider who you want to bless today with loving and lovely words.

*Lord, help me to hold my tongue and to think and pray before responding when I've been hurt by another. Let my choice of words be blameless so that I honor You. Give me patience and the strength to choose language that builds up others.*

# What Children Need

~·~

"*T*here's no way my kids will sit still for family devotions! I tried it once and it was a disaster." Sometimes your biggest frustrations can be resolved when you take a look at them from another angle. Proverbs 13:24 says that if you love your children, you will teach them. And like discipline, the earlier the better.

Moms tell me all the time, "My children don't want to have devotions. They don't want to sit and listen to me read the Bible or Bible storybooks." My answer is always the same: Give your children what they *need*, not what they *want*. You're the mom. You know what's best. My thinking goes like this: God says to train them; therefore, I train them! Becoming a woman who is obedient to her heavenly Father will help you raise children who are obedient, healthy, and filled with the knowledge that you and God want the very best for them.

*Lord, I have given in under the pressure of my children's moments of wanting and whining. Give me the strength to stand up for what I know is the best for them. And Lord, please give me peace about following through with my convictions.*

# Loving Discipline

*D*o you have a child who has decided to live out the "terrible twos" for many years? I've been there, believe me. But don't give up. The Bible says when you spare discipline, you actually show hate to a child (Proverbs 13:24). So if you love a child, you'll discipline promptly. Take comfort in the truth that our heavenly Father corrects those He loves, those "in whom he delights" (Proverbs 3:12).

And why do we correct children? Because discipline brings wisdom and because foolishness is bound up in the heart of a child. Children will protest, cry, squirm, argue, and emote. It goes with the territory. Plan and prepare for their protests so you won't be swayed to change your response. Following through with your parenting responsibilities isn't always comfortable, but there is great reward for you and your child when you do so.

*God, I want my children to respect me and their father. I also want them to know the importance of relying on Your authority for their choices. Help me be a mom of my word so that I model faithfulness in all of my actions—especially when it is difficult.*

# The Real Thing

*If* your children aren't eager to say their prayers at night or read their Bibles, it might be time to take a look at your own faithfulness in those areas. Actions *do* speak louder than words, and children catch on very quickly. It's so important to live out a genuine faith before them, for then you establish credibility, and you create a foundation for teaching God's Word.

If you want your children to love God and follow His ways, then you must let them see *you* love God and follow Him. Second Timothy 1:3-5 shines light on the impact a mother and grandmother of faith can have: "I remember you in my prayers night and day…when I call to remembrance the genuine faith that is in you, which dwelt first in your grandmother Lois and your mother Eunice." Timothy was a godly man because the women in his family honored their faith. May this be true of your legacy.

*Father, show me how to be a light for my children. Guide my steps so that I guide their steps toward Your heart and will. It gives me joy today to think of the ways that my children might honor You with their futures, lives, and prayers.*

# True Beauty

*T*wo Christian moms talked about a show they'd seen featuring teenagers saving money for cosmetic surgeries. Sadly, as the women discussed the topic, it became clear they had the same frustrations as the teen girls did about their appearances. They had the same trouble accepting themselves as beautiful. I don't think that's a mere coincidence. The negative attitudes adult women have about their bodies and looks are affecting how young girls see their bodies.

I want you to believe in your beauty and your value. Ephesians 2:10 reminds us that "we are His workmanship, created in Christ Jesus for good works, which God prepared beforehand that we should walk in them." You are the lovely work of God's hands. Trust that true beauty is all about your heart. And let the young women in your life know this too.

*God, teach me to see my beauty through Your eyes. Help me let go of discontentment about my appearance. Give me the desire to treat my body as a temple and to treat my life as creation for good works through Christ.*

# Beauty from the Heart

*B*eauty begins in the heart, inside a woman, at her very core. May your prayer be, "Lord, grant that I may become inwardly beautiful." The wise woman after God's own heart seeks to be noticed not for clothing or jewelry, or a good figure, but for kind and good character. Don't neglect your outward appearance; just make sure there's a godly balance. First Timothy 2:9-10 exhorts women to "adorn themselves in modest apparel, with propriety and moderation, not with braided hair or gold or pearls or costly clothing, but, which is proper for women professing godliness, with good works."

It's not bad to stay fit, eat healthy, manage your weight, and dress in good taste. Just don't let outward appearance become an obsession that undermines the godliness and loveliness that are born of the heart.

*Lord, let my good works and kindness be what people notice first about me. When I'm discouraged about my physical appearance, help me choose ways to improve my health from the inside out. I want my loveliness to be pleasing to You.*

# All to the Glory of God

*If 'we are what we eat,' then consider me an extra helping of chocolate cookie dough." Oh, how I relate to that. I remember all too well a phase in my life when I tried to deal with everything by drinking colas and eating candy, cookies, and yes, even chocolate cookie dough. I was a physical mess—a junk food addict. Has this happened to you? Maybe unhealthy food choices are a part of your struggle right now?

First Corinthians 10:31 puts an incredible spin on our eating habits. It says, "Therefore, whether you eat or drink, or whatever you do, do all to the glory of God." Think about that for a second. God has spoken about how we should eat and drink. He's given us His wisdom in practical and meaningful ways. When the temptations are great, feed your soul with God's principles for your life.

> *Lord, You've seen me struggle with my choices when it comes to eating and drinking. Help me embrace Your principles. Today, I surrender this specific area of life to Your will so that I fill my hunger with Your wisdom and hope.*

# Discipline—a Good Thing

*D*iscipline. It can be a scary word. Many women associate discipline with losing control of their choices. It relates to not eating this, or only doing that, or following godly guidance. It is true that you might limit some of your choices if you're obedient to God, but the tradeoff is actually *freedom*. When you give over your daily choices to godly discipline in every area of your life, you experience the freedom of righteous living.

Discipline in every area of life is important. You know this, but do you understand why? Your life has a positive or negative effect on everyone you live with, know, or encounter. That's a significant influence. Galatians 5:22-23 says that self-control and self-discipline are among the manifestations of God's Spirit working in your life—a *good* thing! And when you struggle with discipline, trust in the Lord and give your new godly habits time. You'll be amazed at the transformation in your life.

*Okay, God. It is time for me to stop giving excuses for my lack of discipline. When I bring my thoughts and actions under Your guidance and power, the fruit of the Spirit can grow in my life. I long for this harvest of godly characteristics, and I'm ready to do what it takes.*

# Number Your Days

~·~

*H*mmm. Remember when you thought that age 30 sounded old? In the Bible, Moses speculated our years would be about 70 or 80. You do the math. How old are you today? And approximately how many years do you have left? We don't know the number of our days, but we do know that Psalm 90:12 instructs us to "number our days, that we may gain a heart of wisdom."

Just think what could be accomplished for God and others if you seek a heart of wisdom and walk diligently with God each and every day and throughout all your remaining years. Don't waste away your most important resource, your life. Number your days. And use each and every one of them for God's glory and the good of others.

*Lord, I give You my days. I am inspired to make them count. Each and every day and each and every year. Give me Your eyes, Your heart, and Your desires for this life of mine. I'm starting to see things differently already.*

# A Habit for Life

*I*'m not good at praying, so I just don't do it. Other people are made for it." If you've fallen into this faulty thinking, I want to encourage you to start talking to God. The Bible says *when* you pray, not *if* you pray. So prayer isn't merely optional for a Christian. In Matthew 6, our Lord assumed prayer would be the habit of our lives. He assumed that drawing upon God for spiritual strength is as needful and as natural as breathing.

Decide right now that you'll set aside some time each day alone for prayer. Five minutes, ten minutes…whatever you feel you can start with. Just get started. A passion for prayer is born out of the decisions you make, and a lifetime habit will be born through faithful commitment of your time to talk to your Lord. You won't be sorry. And you'll soon realize that you are made for prayer.

*God, You are here for me. Release me from the obstacles of doubt, shame, and indifference so that I run to You with vulnerability and in anticipation of being embraced and heard by my heavenly Father.*

# Not Your Own

～•～

*T*here is much discussion and debate about a person's rights and ownership of their body. The truth is, as a Christian, your body doesn't belong to you. Those may seem like harsh words and they're definitely not politically correct, but the Bible says your body belongs to your Maker. First Corinthians 6:19 asks, "Do you not know that your body is the temple of the Holy Spirit who is in you, whom you have from God, and you are not your own?"

Believers, both male and female, have been designed by God for His purposes, not our own. You are to be used for His glory, and you're called by God, expected by God, and commanded by God to live in a way that brings honor to Him. That provides a lot of clarity about how we're to live, doesn't it?

*God, You formed me in my mother's womb and You know everything there is to know about me, my body, and my heart. I will give You glory in the way I treat the temple of the Holy Spirit. I love belonging to You.*

# God in Your Heart

~·~

*H*ave you ever wished that your husband had a stronger faith? Have you spent time dwelling on his lack of spiritual growth? Even if his spiritual maturity is lacking, there's another area that needs your attention—*your* heart. Deuteronomy 6:5-6 says, "You shall love the Lord your God with all your heart, with all your soul, and with all your strength. And these words which I command you today shall be in your heart." When you love God with all of your heart and soul, your focus is on your spiritual growth.

Concern yourself with making sure you're a virtuous wife. Be sure that your life is centered on the Lord. By all means, lift up your husband in prayer and be his godly helpmate. And even if there are no changes in your husband or in the tone of your marriage, commit to walking through each day with God's wisdom and grace.

*Father, I will keep my eyes and heart set on You. When I focus on someone else's lack of faith, remind me that You hold that person in Your hand. You call me to work on my spiritual growth. Keep me from prideful or judgmental thoughts so as a godly wife I can build up my husband.*

# Talk Things Over

*V*oicemail, email, and text messages are replacing more in-person conversations—even in marriages. To improve communication with your husband, listen to him. Pay attention to his words and needs. Engage in conversation rather than in arguments or battles for control. Communication is the goal—winning is not.

It's important that you and your husband seek agreement on the main issues that challenge any marriage: finances, raising the children, the daily schedule, your priorities and goals as a couple, and how you spend your evenings, weekends, and vacations. Ephesians 4:26 is a great communication-in-marriage rule: "Do not let the sun go down on your wrath." In other words, don't go to bed angry. Don't turn away from important talks. Kind and loving communication will draw you closer to answers and to each other.

> *Lord, give me open ears and an open heart so I really hear my husband. Renew our desire to tend to each other's needs, hopes, and dreams. And in the tough daily matters, grant us both patience and wisdom.*

# If the Lord Wills It

〜•〜

*W*omen have a lot of choices and opportunities these days. If you know what you want and are moving forward with such force that nothing can stop you…wait! Isn't there something missing in this plan? Isn't someone missing? Even when you have a great plan and lots of experience, you don't have the knowledge that God holds. Nor do you know what the future holds.

In James 4:14, we are told, "You do not know what will happen tomorrow. For what is your life? It is even a vapor that appears for a little time and then vanishes away." You are a puff of smoke, a vapor—but God knows all. When you leave God out of your plans, your sin is one of omission—omitting Him. Pray over your plans, and then say, "Lord willing." After all, only God knows your future. Only He has a purpose for your life. You can make plans, but remember—whatever happens will come about "if the Lord wills" (verse 15).

*If You will it, Lord, these plans I have for tomorrow will unfold and will honor the purpose and path You have shaped for me. I will trust in Your knowledge and strength, and not in my own.*

# Nurturing Friendships

~·~

Friendships take energy and effort to maintain. Sadly, when life gets busy, it can be your friends who don't hear from you for a while—sometimes a long while. You never wake up in the morning and decide, "I think I'll neglect my friends today." It's much more subtle than that. The truth is that friendships must be nurtured to survive. And that takes time, care, and love. It might take a little money and thoughtfulness too, such as finding just the right card, a small gift, or that special something your friend collects or enjoys. It may even mean a trip to another location to sustain a special relationship either with an individual friend or even a couple. As the apostle Paul said of his friends in Philippi, "I have you in my heart." A good friend is like having a "twin sister" in Christ—you're never far from each other in heart.

*Lord, thank You for bringing my dear friends to mind. Give me awareness of their needs and of their great value in my life. May I be a good friend to them and lift them up in prayer. I am grateful for the gift of friendship.*

# Precious Promises

~•~

*I*nstead of becoming a woman of the world, become a woman of her word. It's a far more precious and valued reputation. And you can go to the greatest resource on promises and truth for inspiration. Did you know there are more than 8000 promises in the Bible? Promises you can rely on! In 1 Kings 8:56, Solomon shares the truth about God: "There has not failed one word of all His good promise."

Familiarize yourself with each and every word of your Bible. Count each and every priceless promise of hope. Memorize them and make them your own. Second Peter 1:3-4 says, "His divine power has given to us all things that pertain to life and godliness, through the knowledge of Him who called us by glory and virtue, by which have been given to us exceedingly great and precious promises." Base your life on the promises of the Bible, and you will become a woman who reflects her faithful God.

*Father, do people see You in me and through my actions? I want to be a woman of my word and a woman of Your Word. I will follow Your precious promises through all of my life.*

# 59
# Your Heart's Showing

~•~

Your heart reflects what you and your mind take in. When you turn to your TV more than you turn to God's Word, you and your heart will reflect the drama—and not the entertaining kind. The Twenty-Third Channel goes like this: "The TV is my shepherd. My spiritual growth shall want. It maketh me to sit down and do nothing for its name's sake—because it requireth all my spare time."

You can laugh—and you should! But you also need to be serious about your priorities. The next time you catch yourself talking on and on about a show, or even the news, keep in mind that your heart is showing. Turn off the TV and get on your knees to worship. And schedule some prime time to memorize the beautiful Twenty-Third Psalm. Your heart will show the wonder of God's promises.

*Lord, forgive me for devoting so much time to TV, movies, and other distractions. Draw me to the joy and wonder of Your Word. I want my heart to reflect Your peace and Your grace.*

# Hidden Strength

*A*re you ready to do some soul-searching? As women we simply must examine our hearts. Are you a woman of faithfulness? Can others—beginning with those at home—count on you? Can others trust you with information? With work? With responsibility? Can others place their confidence in you no matter what? Proverbs 25:19 says, "Like a broken tooth or a lame foot is reliance on the unfaithful in a time of trouble" (NIV). Do you want to be a woman who is as unsteady as a broken foot or do you want to be a woman your family can lean on in times of trouble?

You are to be a support to your husband, children, and to those God calls you to serve. And your strength is to come from the Lord. Faithfulness, commitment, obedience, perseverance, and willingness to follow God's lead—let these traits become your hidden strength.

*God, lead me to faithfulness and strength. As I stand in Your presence, I want to examine my heart and find the traits that make me a help and a refuge for my family and for others.*

# Share the Joy

*J*oy multiplies when it's shared. But so many married women reserve the idea of fun for time with their girlfriends rather than their husbands. To spark joy in your marriage, know that it comes from your heart, not from your circumstances. If you face difficulties as a couple, such as financial struggles, stressful jobs, or the rewarding but trying demands of parenting, don't let them override your opportunity to share in laughs, happy memories, and new adventures.

Your thoughts and attitudes make all the difference. Are you fueling memories of events that cause disappointment? Do you have a sad spirit? The ultimate source of all joy is the Lord. Nehemiah 8:10 calls it your strength. Rejoice each day on purpose. Play music. Smile. Share the joy with others. It'll revolutionize your life.

*Lord, I long to see my husband's great smile. I want to be a wife who uplifts my marriage relationship. Change my heart, Lord, and give me the desire to share joy with the love of my life.*

# God's Patience Is Yours

~•~

"Oh I have plenty of patience—as long as everything's going my way!" There are a lot of jokes about patience, but when you're the one forced to wait while you suffer—or suffer while you wait—it's no laughing matter. You can feel your pulse race and your frustration rise. Psalm 27:14 says, "Wait on the LORD; be of good courage, and He shall strengthen your heart."

You may be a woman who walks with God, but you are not courageous *enough*, strong *enough*, on your own. God's strength, however, is more than enough. Is there something God is asking you to be patient about right now? You have to live with "what is." But remember, you have God's promise for "what is to be." Colossians 3:12 says you can either fret, worry, and pace, *or* you can put on a heart of patience. Which will it be for you during this time of waiting?

> *Heavenly Father, I need Your strength. I am impatient and worried as I wait for an answer, a solution, a hope. Today I will rest in Your good and gracious help and embrace Your promise of "what is to be."*

# Sweet Speech

*H*ave you ever received the painful comment "You're a nag" from your husband? That is not the kindest description, but unfortunately there are times when your prompts or lists of projects or barely veiled demands probably come across as harsh. Here's the message: A crabby, cranky, nagging, complaining wife annoys her husband in the same way a constant drip gets on your nerves—and drives you crazy. It can drive a husband away. To the attic, the rooftop, in front of the TV, even to the garage. He'll make excuses to be out of earshot. Have you already experienced this?

Maybe today's the day to make some changes. To take a hard look at yourself. It's worth the pain, believe me. Are you a listener or a whiner? Do your words calm, or do they resemble that dripping faucet? Let your sweet speech mark you as a woman after God's own heart.

*Lord, I have let my speech overflow with commands, complaints, and criticisms. How did I become this person? Help me reconnect with my husband with words of encouragement and kindness. Help me reflect Your heart for him no matter what our circumstances.*

# His Truth

*He's* just not what he appears to be. And there's no one I can share that with." There are problems, and there are problem husbands. But don't give up. Thank God for pastors, counselors, and wise older women who can help with the application of God's principles in your circumstances. Share your situation with one of these wise people.

But in the meantime, and always, you have God's Word to guide you. When in doubt, check it out. It's not just a cute phrase; it's a sincere reminder of what to do daily. What does God have to say about marriage? About trials and hurts and disappointments? You will be helped and blessed each and every time you implement God's truth and follow His instructions.

> *God, when I am looking all around me for help, I'm holding Your guiding light in my hands—Your Word. Lead me to godly people for their wisdom and lead me back to Your guidance for my every concern.*

# More than Gold

~•~

Whether you have a lot of money or you have very little, you can end up letting it take over your thoughts and priorities. But there are more important things than money that deserve your time and focus. For instance, *character*. Your reputation is a higher priority than money. Wisdom is more desirable than money. And humility is better than money.

Here's another twist! You as a godly wife are better than money to your husband. The Bible says, "Houses and riches are an inheritance from fathers, but a prudent wife is from the LORD" (Proverbs 19:14). In fact, a godly wife is a husband's greatest asset. With a godly wife of character, humility, wisdom, and faithfulness beside him, the Bible says your husband will have no lack of gain. Why? Because as a virtuous wife, your worth is far above rubies (Proverbs 3:10-11).

*Father, let me seek my value as a woman of character. Show me where I am poor in spirit so that I can invest in all that matters to You. Let my character always make my husband feel wealthy in ways that matter.*

# Talking with God

~·~

*I* don't pray because I feel like God doesn't really know me. Why should He?"

Do you ever feel like this? We all have difficulty talking with a stranger. So the solution is obvious. It is time to get to know God better. Talk to God through prayer. Actively seek to close the distance between you and your Lord. As one of my favorite verses, James 4:8, instructs, "Draw near to God and He will draw near to you." It's really that simple.

What are some of the behaviors or attitudes that are creating distance in your relationship with God? Neglect? Bitterness? Laziness? Sin? I'm sure you can add to the list. Just think about any friendship or former friendship that isn't as close as it used to be. What happened? Make a step now to reconnect with God. Draw near to the one friend you'll have for eternity.

*Lord, I love You and I want to be close to You. I will draw near to Your heart through prayer and through the reading of Your Word. Your presence is my comfort and Your love is my hope.*

# 67
# Be a Woman of God

～•～

*H*ave you been on the fast track for some time? I'm all for a successful career—but careers are soon over. Titles or promotions come and go. But what you do for others will have a lasting impact. Whether you're married or single, your ministry to and with God's people has lasting benefits. Read the story of Miriam in Deuteronomy. She was a woman of considerable achievements. She was also a remarkable woman who loved God, her family, and God's people. She served them with all her heart, soul, mind, and strength.

Philippians 4:8 instructs us, "Whatever things are noble…whatever things are lovely, whatever things are of good report, if there is any virtue and if there is anything praiseworthy—meditate on these things." Become all of these things and make it a lifetime pursuit.

*Father, I've always strived to be a woman who honors a strong work ethic. Now I understand how much I need to strive to be a woman of godly honor. I want to be noble, lovely, of good report, and praiseworthy.*

# God's Perfect Design

~·~

$\mathcal{M}$irror, mirror on the wall—who's the fairest of them all?" Okay, that's a dramatic line from a fairy tale. But have you ever compared yourself to other women with a sigh of dismay or discouragement? I say revel in your womanhood, your femaleness. Why not? There's no need to feel inferior, subpar, or second-rate. Woman was God's last, most beautiful creation. It was only after God presented woman that He proclaimed His creation was "very good."

Read the stories of women in the Bible. Allow God's truth to permeate your understanding and transform your view of yourself, and other women, until it matches the high value God places on you. As God's woman, be the best of the best. Delight in God's perfect design and plan for your life. What a great joy. You don't need a fairy tale drama or ending to tell you who is beautiful and valued. You are God's precious creation.

*Father, You made me. There is no other compliment, endorsement, or word of encouragement I need to hear or know. Keep me from the negative desire to compare myself to anyone. May I embrace my identity in You and my beauty as Your daughter.*

# Get Some Rest

*A*re you running on empty? Do you need coffee and late nights at the computer to catch up? I have a helpful bit of wisdom to share with you. It may sound impossible, but you've got to get more rest. I try to head for the bedroom around 7:00 in the evening to begin those nighttime rituals early. I look at my planner, jot down some notes, and take care of a few other no-brainer activities. I don't start anything that will cause me to stay up late worrying or working.

What can *you* do to get to bed earlier? Eliminate some television? Cut your caffeine intake? Get the kids to bed sooner? Something is better than nothing—no matter how small that something is. You can't expect to grow in your spiritual walk with the Lord if fatigue is the rule of your day. Get some rest. Your body, mind, and spirit will thank you. And I'll bet that your family and friends will too.

*Lord, I need Your rest and Your peace. Release me from my worries and the bad habits that trigger sleepless nights and low-energy days. I will give my concerns over to You in prayer, and I will seek Your strength and comfort.*

# Order Your Behavior

~•~

*T*he programs about home organization are a big hit. The problem is that more people are probably watching shows about ordering their lives than actually following through with the advice. Good news is here: Management skills can be learned *and* applied to make your life better. I'm a living, walking testimony and an *organized* one.

But I warn you it'll take time. I love the adage that reminds us, "Life is what happens to you while you're failing to plan it." That was me. So I started asking for help, reading books, using a planner. Titus 2:5 is a great incentive. It encourages you to order your behavior so that the Word of God is not blasphemed. In other words, a woman who walks with God honors God in the way she manages her home. Don't miss out on the blessing of a happy home.

> *God, give me the perspective, motivation, and direction of Your priorities so that I can see how and where to begin. I want my home to bring You honor and to give my family the peace of order.*

# Doing Your Work Heartily

~·~

*W*hat's your attitude like? Colossians 3:23 says, "Whatever you do, do it heartily." *Heartily.* That's not a word you hear very often these days, and that's too bad. Because it means giving your work everything you've got. And "heartily" doing that work as to the Lord, not for anyone else who may be watching. Have you put in extra effort so that others will notice or compliment you? It's good to serve others with your absolute best, but let your motivation always be to please the Lord and not to receive accolades.

A God-focused attitude is positive and directs you to better the lives of those you love while giving God the glory. So, how's your attitude?

*Lord, I like the idea of living and giving heartily. There is energy and purpose behind work done to honor You. Show me where my attitude needs improvement and I will be diligent about making changes. I want to give You my all.*

# Time for a Change

~•~

*I*f you've felt on edge lately, maybe it's time for a change of manner and demeanor. You can transform yourself into a woman of contentment and joy. A woman who extends grace to others and to herself. Does this sound good? You have all the resources of a mighty and powerful God to help you make it happen. Prayer. The truths of Scripture. Not to mention the sweet strength of God's fruit of the Spirit.

Discover the inspiring list in Galatians 5:22-23: "The fruit of the Spirit is love, joy, peace, longsuffering, kindness, goodness, faithfulness, gentleness, self-control." Doesn't just reading that list smooth those edges and bring calm to your soul? The only question is—*will* you embrace this change? Believe me, when God makes your heart tender toward His will, it'll make a difference in your outlook, life, and in all your relationships.

*God, I don't want my weariness and my frustration to become who I am. This heart of mine is ready to surrender to the changes only You can make happen. I long to have the abundance of the fruit of the Spirit.*

# Faithful in All Things

~•~

*T*o pursue God's heart sounds great, but what does it look like? Scripture says a woman must be faithful in all things. To *know* God's will is a woman's greatest treasure. To *do* His will is life's greatest privilege. Have you ever viewed living out God's best in your life as a privilege? It truly is. Discipline, commitment, obedience—those sound like words of duty, but they are the actions that usher you to the blessing of living a godly life.

Our priorities as seen in Titus 2:3-5 are to love God, love our husband, and love our children. And married or single, to love our home, and to love and serve God's people. Serving others is an important assignment directly from God; therefore, it comes *before* and ranks *higher* in priority than a personal goal or the pursuit of security. Seek to be filled by fulfilling God's will.

*I call on You today, Lord, with a desire to know and do Your will. Shape my heart to be like Your own. Lead me to Your priorities and help me to release my hold on personal ambitions that do not fit Your purpose for me.*

# Give It Your All

~•~

With my laptop I can work on emails wherever I go. Isn't technology wonderful? The difficulty is when it comes time to turn off those convenient devices. And there is a time to do that! When your work day's over, be sure it's *over*. Leave work at work. This is important for both single and married women. Healthy habits are for all women. So leave the disputes and emotions of the job behind so that your home life gets your devoted attention.

If you're married with children, be sure that you set this boundary so that you are fully present for them. Your husband is the most important person in your life. He deserves a listening ear and a pleasant evening. Before you say, "What about *me?*" let me remind you—right now we're talking about how to become a godly woman. If you give God your all, you'll enjoy your family and your life to the max. Soak up every pleasure that home and family bring to your heart.

*Lord, I confess that I dive into the constant stream of work and online visits with friends instead of being with my family. Guide me to make healthy boundaries. I truly desire the connection of focused conversation and family time. Help me fulfill this desire with godly behavior.*

# Creative Fun

~·~

"When we were dating, John came up with the best dates. Ah, the good ol' days! Long gone. I'm talkin' long gone." Does this sound like something you have said or thought? If you're longing for the husband who sits around dreaming up romantic outings and extraordinary events, this is your wake-up call. Since when do you have to wait for your husband to come up with all the fun ideas? Women are creative and clever. Nothing says you can't be the initiator in the fun department. Go ahead, make some plans. A picnic, a romantic dinner by candlelight, a night out doing something he might enjoy doing. I guarantee, your husband will show up and he will enjoy it. Be creative and let your lively, lovely spirit show. You'll both be so glad you did.

*God, give my husband and me times of refreshment and reconnection. We both need time together and a reminder that joy and laughter and relaxation are important for our marriage. May we praise You for the love we share.*

# Pray over Your Calendar

~·~

*A*re you up for a special spiritual assignment? It will transform your prayer life. For the next week, look over and pray over your calendar of events. I want you to pay particular attention to the needs of your family or those closest to you. On each day of the next week, mark the exact time you'll designate as your prayer time. It can be the same time each day, or you can make it fit the demands and schedule of each day. Put your prayer appointments in ink or in bold if you're using a computer. The most important step is to keep these appointments with God. You don't just forget a dental appointment, or blow off a hair appointment. How much more important is your time with God? To *not* take time to pray is to leave God out of your life.

> *Lord, my heart is hungry for You. I promise to schedule time with You and to follow through. It's exciting to put You first.*

# Sounding the Alarm

~·~

*H*as your husband said no to something that you had planned on adding to your schedule? If so, be glad he speaks up—on *your* behalf, by the way. Believe me, Jim has said no many times. Your husband can be key to helping you keep your priorities straight. If he sounds the alarm when things are out of balance, consider yourself a blessed woman. His direction is a way that God guides you. So when Jim suggests that I think twice before taking on a commitment, I thank God for him. And if he sees that it is not a good or godly direction, I decline the opportunity, whatever it may be, without a bitter bone in my body. Following God's will that I follow my husband's leadership keeps me and my service in the center of God's will. It's a nice feeling to be centered.

*Lord, may I have a heart willing to listen to my husband's input. Thank You for speaking to me through his guidance and his desire for my very best.*

# The Answer to Trouble

~.~

*W*hat difficulties are you experiencing during this season of your life? I sympathize with you. John 16:33 says, "I have told you these things, so that in me you may have peace. In this world you will have trouble. But take heart! I have overcome the world" (NIV).

Trouble is a fact of life. And a fact of faith is that you can ease your trouble with prayer. Prayer releases the energy of God. Ask God to do what you cannot do. Don't cave in. And don't suffer. There's hope in James 5:13: "Is anyone among you in trouble? Let them pray. Is anyone happy? Let them sing songs of praise" (NIV). I've had to learn that as I praise God for the highlights in my life, I must also pray to Him for the trials and troubles. The Bible says He will fight your battles. He will judge and make things right. Don't lose heart—just bring your heart before God.

> *Lord, I have carried the weight of these troubles for so long. I want to give them to You. I know that You make things right through Your redemption and grace. And You do what I cannot do—make things new and right.*

# Forgive and Pray

~·~

*I*f you struggle to pray for someone who has hurt you, it is time to take your wounds and that person to God in prayer. Yes, it's difficult to forgive someone who's failed you as a friend. But if you don't, you give up the opportunity to minister to that person *through* prayer. James 5:16 states, "Confess your trespasses to one another, and pray for one another, that you may be healed. The effective, fervent prayer of a righteous man avails much." This means that your heart must be right before God in order to forgive and to pray for those who fail or have failed you. It's natural for you to want to write that person off, but God's Word says you're to forgive one another as God in Christ forgave you. So forgive and pray. It takes a lot of maturity to simply forgive. And a lot of healing takes place when you do.

*Heavenly Father, You know the person I have trouble praying for. I forgive them for the hurt they've caused me. And today I ask for forgiveness for the times when my heart has been hardened. I want to experience the freedom of forgiving and being forgiven.*

# Confessing Sin

~•~

*T*here is a test that reveals the condition of your heart. No, it isn't an EKG; it is the test of how you handle your mistakes. Are you stubborn? Do you stand your ground even when you're wrong? It's hard to admit when you've messed up. It's hurtful. And it's embarrassing! But I've learned that when you admit to mistakes, ask for prayer, and seek forgiveness, the condition of your situation—and of your heart—greatly improves.

In Psalm 32, David expressed the incredible benefits of confessing our sins: "Day and night your hand was heavy on me; my strength was sapped as in the heat of summer. Then I acknowledged my sin to you and did not cover up my iniquity. I said, 'I will confess my transgressions to the LORD.' And You forgave the guilt of my sin" (NIV). The Lord calls you to admit your sin and to pray always. You'll slip up again. We all do. Use your next sin as a chance to grow as a woman of God.

*God, I blew it. I was wrong and didn't want to admit it. Show me how to release my pride so that my heart is humble and eager to seek forgiveness from You and from others.*

# First Things First

*If* your to-do list never ends, or worse yet, never even begins, there is something to put first on that list. Put first things first, no matter how busy you are. Try giving God the first minutes of each day. Read a chapter from your favorite book in the Bible or a part of Scripture you've never explored. Pray for direction and strength.

Proverbs 3:9 instructs you and me to honor the Lord with the "firstfruits" of all that we've been given. And the promised result is that you'll be filled with plenty.

You'll be blessed in your spirit and your practical life when you make it a point to give God the first things of each fresh new day. Make your appointment with Him the initial act of your day, and you'll be surprised how much more of your to-do list you'll accomplish the rest of the day.

*Lord, how long have I put off putting You first? I want You to be the center of my life, and I know that means You are to be the start of my day. My first thoughts. My first actions. I give them to You as my offering of praise.*

# The Bible Is Alive

~·~

*I*f it seems like you have more failures than successes, there's a way you can turn that around. The Bible is "living and powerful" (Hebrews 4:12), and it will speak straight to your heart. You may not want to think about this, but as you read God's Word, it'll point out behaviors and attitudes and practices that don't match up with God's desire for your life. You'll also discover that the world's version of success varies greatly from God's measure of success.

Let Him teach you the way to go. Martin Luther said, "The Bible is alive, it speaks to me; it has feet, it runs after me; it has hands, it lays hold on me." God's Word also has the power to mend you and move you forward. After you've fallen and failed, God's Word picks you up, brushes you off, and builds you up.

*God, let the power of Your Word shed light on my weaknesses, sins, and misconceptions. I want to walk in Your truth so that Your Word is alive in me and is evident in my life. Thank You for mending my brokenness and leading the way forward.*

# Open Your Heart

~·~

*W*hy pray? You can probably list lots of reasons that sound spiritual and wise, but do you ever just wake up and think, *What's the point?* If this is you right now, think about this: The point of prayer is to point you to God. When your focus is elsewhere, your heart can become hardened and resistant to His leading. You so desperately need a soft, flexible heart so you don't miss God's message to you.

As a woman of God, you need God's help in order to live your life His way. Jeremiah 17:9 says our heart is wicked—just in case you hadn't already discovered that fact. But through prayer you open up your heart to God. And when you do, He searches you, exposes your motives, and gives you the opportunity to bring your will in line with His plan. That sounds wonderful to me! How about *you*, my friend?

> *Yes, Lord, I've built up walls around my heart because I've been discouraged. You call me to seek You and to point my heart, attention, and hope toward You and You alone. Thank You for being here for me, Lord.*

# Let the Adventure Begin

~·~

"As a woman I'm to be moderate, temperate, disciplined…and boring!" No, no, no. It's time to dispel the myth that the Christian walk requires you to be bland and uninteresting. Not on your life. God wants nothing to have control over you. Instead, you're to have control over everything.

The Christian life is a powerful and exciting existence. And God provides the grace so you can say no to those things that don't fit this godly life. Try it. The next time you want a second helping of food, pass it up. The next time you want to sleep in, get up. The next time you're distracted from the goals God has given you, say no. Stick to God's plan. And that calls for discipline of life and soul. Make those good, better, and best choices. Follow God's lead, and you are in for one great adventure.

*God, I admit that I have focused on the idea of rules more than ruling over areas of my life. Through Your grace, I have strength and ability and a future. There's nothing boring about a life of purpose.*

# Start Walking

*A*re you out there moving? If you've been miss-ing out on the benefits of a good walk, don't wait another day. The rewards are great. Believe it or not, with a little walking a couple of times a week, you'll sleep better and feel better. And yes, this is part of a godly, healthy lifestyle. When my body was about at its worst, I began walking. The changes I experienced were so positive that I made walking a regular part of my life.

Whether you take a stroll or make your way around the neighborhood at a good pace, it's a glo-rious time to spend with God and His creation, rain or shine. Maybe walking for exercise is a disci-pline—a goal—you want for your life. Then pray. Pray about your life. Pray about your body. Pray about your energy level. And pray about your pro-ductivity. There's nothing wrong with disciplining your physical life. In moderation, it can also make your spiritual life more vibrant.

*I'm setting a walking date with You, Lord. I want to be renewed and refreshed. Give me the energy I need to get started. Fill me with wonder as I breathe in the fresh air, feel my body in motion, and pay attention to Your creation.*

# The "Outer" Woman

*S*arah was called a beautiful woman by her husband, Abraham, in Genesis 12:11. Both Rebekah and Rachel were described as beautiful of form and face. And Queen Esther was called "exquisite"—she was a woman who obtained favor in the sight of all who saw her. There are ways you can take care of your appearance so that the "outer" woman looks her best.

Caring for your appearance has a place, but don't let it become a worry or an obsession. You look exactly as God meant you to look. Make the effort to *fix up* what you have with a little makeup now and then. *Dress up* with clothes that fit nicely and make you feel good. *Shape up* with an exercise routine that gives your body strength and energy.

And tend to that heart of yours. The best beauty treatment of all is time spent quietly before the Lord.

*God, thank You for making me the person I am… with this body, mind, heart, and soul. Your love is my beauty secret. Help me to be a woman who is viewed as a woman of loveliness.*

# A Steady Pace

～·～

Keeping up with the hectic pace of life can become disheartening. If this is how you are feeling these days, I want to encourage you with some refreshing thoughts from God's Word. I have some favorite verses I'd love to share. These give me a second wind when I'm feeling worn out or discouraged. In 2 Timothy 4:7, Paul said, "I have fought the good fight, I have finished the race, I have kept the faith." And then in 1 Corinthians 15:58, Paul wrote, "My beloved brethren, be steadfast, immovable, always abounding in the work of the Lord, knowing that your labor is not in vain in the Lord."

The Christian life isn't a spurt or a sputter. It's not to be a life characterized by false starts. Life management in Christ is like a marathon—a long, sustained, steady pace. And the prize is a life of dedication and service to God. Be encouraged today—God is with you every step of the journey.

*God, why do I try to rush through everything when You call me to keep my faith and be steadfast in the longer race? Each day of my life is of value to the entire journey. I pray for strength for today and encouragement for tomorrow.*

# Love Your Husband

~·~

*H*ave you ever had a day when you wished you were single again? Marriage is such a gift. It is also a bit of work. So, roll up your sleeves and get busy loving your husband. Show him your love. Lavish him with your love. Show him the kind of attention you'd show to a best friend. After all, your heart and affection should echo that of the Bible in Solomon 5:16: "This is my beloved, and this is my friend."

When your husband is sad, cheer him. When he's noble, praise him. When he's generous, appreciate him. When he's talkative, listen to him. And when he leaves or returns, kiss him! Proverbs 4:23 warns, "Keep your heart with all diligence, for out of it spring the issues of life." Invest in your relationship with your beloved and friend. And be ever so grateful for the labor and treasures of a marriage.

*Lord, I need my heart and attitude to be in line with and in support of my husband. Show me how to be generous with kindness, affection, compliments, support, and love. And give me eyes that watch for the many gifts of married life.*

# Godly Adult in Training

~•~

$T$he Bible says to train up a child in the way he should go. That's a big responsibility, but God doesn't ask you to do it alone. He and His Word are here to help you. The years of a child's life go by so quickly that you can easily fall into a pattern of letting things slide. But keep in mind that you are not just raising a child, but you are training up a future godly adult who will either know or not know how to depend on God, trust His teachings, and walk the Christian path.

Consistently teach God's Word and enforce it with loving discipline. Your children desperately need your faithful training. If they are left on their own, they're going to develop sinful habits and practices. Ephesians 6:4 clearly says to "bring them up in the training and instruction of the Lord" (NIV). It's never too early or too late to do this.

*Heavenly Father, guard my heart from becoming casual with the task of teaching my child Your truths, instructions, and wisdom. As I focus on my child's upbringing today, I also pray for the person of God they will become.*

# True Soul Friends

~•~

*F*inding a good shopping friend is one thing, but finding a sister of the soul is much more difficult. It's so important to have a woman friend to talk with about faith, prayer, hopes, doubts, and your other needs as a believer.

There's nothing better in the world than a friend who's headed in the same direction spiritually. I don't know about you, but I want those friends who are closest to me to know God and to understand the power of prayer.

I want that special person to be someone I can support and delight in, and one who will do the same for me. A friend who believes that when loyalty is called for, loyalty is given. When protection is needed, protection is given. When correction is crucial, correction is given. I want my closest friends to be part of the family of God—true soul friends.

*Lord, lead me to a kindred spirit who is a lover of Your heart and who will be a great companion for my own Christian walk. Help me stay faithful in prayer for this special person, and may I be a friend of the soul.*

# Never Keep Score

*D*o you find it difficult to forgive? I'll never forget the day I discovered the true meaning of one of the verses in the Bible's "love" chapter. First Corinthians 13:5 says that love "thinks no evil." I've read that many times and thought I knew what it meant. But underneath the surface is a surprising message. That love "thinks no evil" means it never totals up the wrongs.

True friends don't keep account of failures or offenses. Understand and support your friends and your family members. Offer them grace. Be thrilled when they succeed. Forgive them when they fail you. And be sure to give without expecting anything in return. Waiting for a kindness to be reciprocated is the same as keeping score. Be a woman of unsurpassed grace—God's kind of grace.

> *God, help me to follow Your model of grace. Forgive me for keeping track of what others do or don't do. Let my focus be on You and my own behavior. I am accountable for my heart, and I don't ever want to be stingy with my love.*

# Memorize Scripture

~•~

$M$ind control is something from a scary movie. But control over your mind and thoughts is a part of godliness. It takes effort, but it's definitely possible through the storing up of God's Word. My greatest treasures are the Bible verses I've memorized over the years. No matter where I am or what's happening in my life, I can pull out and examine one of my treasures. Each gem gives me what I need, and it is straight from God's heart to mine.

"Jesus said, 'You shall love the Lord your God with all your heart, with all your soul, and with all your mind'" (Matthew 22:37). Memorizing Scripture inspires your heart, nurtures your soul, and devotes your mind to all that matters to God. Start simply, but start today. And then keep up the good work…and great thoughts.

*Lord, I want to fill my mind with Your Word. I want to be able to pull up Your truths and promises in a split second. What a comfort and a light that will be for my Christian walk. The message of Scripture is my greatest treasure.*

# Be Selective

~•~

*I*t just slipped out. I'm not in the habit of using profanity—it just happened!" Accidents happen, even in our speaking. But did you know Scripture says, "A good man out of the good treasure of his heart brings forth good; and an evil man out of the evil treasure of his heart brings forth evil. For out of the abundance of the heart his mouth speaks" (Luke 6:45)?

So, what is in your heart will come out in your speech. It's as simple as asking yourself: Do I want to live a godly life? It's important to remind yourself what your priorities are. If your response is "Yes!" then choose to put the things into your mind that lead to living a godly life. Do you want to have a powerful ministry? Then choose to put the things into your mind that can lead to that. Be careful and selective, for God's plan and purposes for your life are extraordinary.

*God, let the words of my mouth be pleasing to You. When I turn to Your Word and direct my path toward the priorities You've shown to me, I will bring honor to You through my words and actions.*

# Doing God's Will

When I see a woman juggling too many activities at once, I can't help but think of Ephesians 5:15, which says, "See then that you walk circumspectly, not as fools but as wise, redeeming the time." As a wise woman, you are to dedicate your life to knowing and doing God's will.

When you place God's Word and prayer time at the center of your life, managing the minutes, hours, and days will come much easier. Why? Because you'll be traveling in God's direction, toward God's will. Instead of struggling against God and His plans and purposes for you, you'll be seeking to do His work His way. Redeem your time with passion and purpose, and you can trade the juggling act for acts of God's wisdom.

*Lord, Your wisdom awaits my attention. I allow distractions and my life goals to fill my time and my thoughts. I've created a life of chaos. I am ready to exchange the way of a fool for the way of a godly, wise woman. Redeem my life, Lord.*

# Pray Through Your Priorities

*D*eciding what to say yes to and what to say no to is not a simple thing. I'm as social as the next person, but I did discover that when I had children at home and I was committed to raising them with God's priorities in mind, I had to determine where other activities, commitments, and people fit within the big picture.

Your family is the masterpiece you're assigned by God to create and to preserve. Beyond that, you are to be very discerning. Each opportunity or event presented as a possibility must be weighed against God's best for your family. That, my friend, takes wisdom.

You must go to the Father of your time and ask Him how much time should be spent with social activities and friendships. Ask Him to spell out what the need of the moment is. Then follow His leading.

*Father, what must I do today to accomplish Your will? What must I let go of or decline in order to preserve my family as a priority? Give me a discerning heart that measures every opportunity against Your will for my family's health.*

# It's the Little Things

*I* just don't have the kind of time it takes for meaningful Bible reading. So why bother?" Little things can make a big difference. Even if you aren't carving out time for an in-depth study of God's Word, *something* is better than nothing. Do you have five minutes a day? That's about how long it takes to read one chapter in your Bible. Start with that. You'll soon find your time growing right along with your spiritual life.

I know you're busy, but you should never be too busy to take care of your spiritual growth. The discipline will be worth it when you experience the joy of growing in the Lord. Take a minute today. On paper, tell God about your desire to grow spiritually. Those few moments could set in motion the direction for the rest of your life.

*Small steps, Lord. I can do small steps. Direct me in my time spent reading Scripture. I am excited to grow spiritually and to draw closer to You each and every day.*

# A First-rate Marriage

~•~

*H*ave you ever scrutinized your husband's efforts, skills, parenting, occupation? Have you ever compared him to a friend's husband in those areas? Wait a minute! Instead of rating your husband, maybe you need to check your own score in the wife department. Are you following God's plan for a wife and helpmate? Are there any gaps in your marriage that can be attributed to your neglect? Any tensions you create?

God's recipe for a happy, first-rate marriage requires you to help, submit, respect, and love. Your assignment from God is not to change your husband, but to warm up his life with your love, improve his life as a helper, follow his leadership with a willing heart. And esteem him highly with utmost respect. So, how do you rate?

*God, when I pay attention to how I am doing, there isn't room to criticize and judge others. Let my focus be on my walk with You. Help me love and support my husband. Give me the eyes to see the potential and hope in my marriage.*

# Touching Lives

~·~

*I* might as well have slept the day away—for all the good I did!" The days do slip away so easily, don't they? When you go to bed at night do you sometimes think over the waking hours and wonder if you've done more harm than good? It's discouraging to believe you didn't make a dent in your plans or an impact on anyone else in a positive way.

God wants His very best for your life. He wants each treasure of a day to be full of goodness that you share with others. If it is evening, plan for tomorrow to count in new and meaningful ways. If it is morning as you read this, plan to move forward right now and share the inspiration of your life with others in big and small ways (they all matter). Go touch lives with the love, grace, and power of Christ.

*Jesus, help me show others the kindness and beauty of Your heart. I want to be a vessel filled with Your words and love so that I overflow with the desire to touch the lives of others. Grant me Your compassion and inspiration to make a difference today.*

# Sweet Speech

~•~

*F*ast talk, sarcasm, and banter can be fun. That would be something I would do if I didn't continually ask God to "sweeten" my speech. I can verbally spar with the best of them, but is that what God is asking of a godly woman? Turning toward words that build up and lift up yourself and others will bring praise to God. Those words will also bring a gladness that surpasses the momentary satisfaction of winning an argument.

It isn't easy to hold your tongue. Ask God for His help in curbing rampant, destructive, and ungodly speech. Proverbs 12:18 tells us, "There is one who speaks like the piercings of a sword, but the tongue of the wise promotes health." If you want to be wise, restrain your lips. Just say nothing. Try it for a day. It'll be difficult, but it will be a day marked by wisdom—a day of glorious victory, peace, and self-control.

*Father, hold me back from speaking the sharp words that come so quickly to my mind. Give me Your thoughts and wisdom. Let my speech be sweet and encouraging. I know it is my life and heart that will be greatly blessed.*

# Beware of Greed

~·~

*A*dmiration for the possessions of others can cloud our gratitude and our priorities. As Christians we're to beware of greed and the love of money. First Timothy 6:18 gets to the heart of a godly woman's purposes: "Do good, that they be rich in good works, ready to give, willing to share." Management of the money and blessings God entrusts to you is a spiritual issue and requires spiritual disciplines and character.

*Give* because God asks you to. *Save* because it will benefit your family. *Budget* because it helps map the path for your lifestyle. *Do without* because a lot of spiritual disciplines are birthed when you sacrifice. And the result is that you'll grow in contentment. Honor the Lord with your possessions and with your money. Give Him the first—and the best.

*Lord, give me the peace of contentment. Guard my heart from greed and ungratefulness. Show me how to give out of a sense of abundance and to manage my resources with wisdom so that I am a good steward of every gift that comes from Your hand.*

# Living in a Christlike Manner

~•~

"*H*ow am I supposed to have this great spiritual life or a strong marriage when my husband isn't a believer?" If this is you, friend, you might have moments when you think it is your responsibility to save your husband. To transform his heart. When you love someone, this is understandable. But your job is not to *be* God, but to *be* Christlike. Only God can change your husband, and only God can save him. Both results occur by a supernatural work that only God can accomplish.

Your assignment is to love, follow, assist, and minister to your non-Christian husband while living in a Christlike manner before his eyes. That's not a popular message, but it doesn't change the fact that it's true. God can help you do anything, including love an unbeliever. Release hold of the responsibilities that belong to God and take joy in being a loving, honorable wife.

*Jesus, change me to become more like You. I pray for my husband—for his life and purpose. And I rest in the comfort of knowing Your care for him is great. Guide me toward behavior that gives You honor and glory, Lord.*

# Serving Others

~•~

Some women worry that they lack the education, ability, or time to minister to others. Don't be one of these women—you'll miss out on some wonderful opportunities God has for you today. You can serve others right where you are. One way is to get in the habit of saying yes when your neighbors invite you to do something. Make it a point to attend the jewelry party, or the neighborhood block party. If someone's child is having a birthday, participate. Your neighbors need to know you're vitally interested in them. Don't be so wrapped up in your church that you're perceived as distant or aloof. Open your home. Have school moms to your house for coffee and cake and a gab session. Hospitality is a great gift to give others. Make a list of the things you'd feel comfortable doing, and then get at it.

*God, guide me toward chances to minister through neighborly kindness and hospitality. Help me open up my heart and home to people who are a part of my world. Give me a servant's perspective in all that I do.*

# 103
# Necessary Food

~·~

You pay immediate attention to your physical hunger, but when your spiritual life needs nourishment, do you ignore it? The food is right there for us. Job 23:12 says, "I have not departed from the commandment of His lips; I have treasured the words of His mouth more than my necessary food." God's Word is food for your *soul*.

How often do you eat? Daily, of course. How often should you go to the Word of God for wisdom? Daily. Take it one day at a time. Just for today, read your Bible. It'll stir your soul and encourage your heart. At the rate of ten minutes a day, you can read through the whole Bible in a year. Tomorrow, continue what you began today. If you're faithful just for this week, you'll be well on your way to making a habit that will bring eternal benefits. Be wise. Invest your time in something that lasts forever.

*God, I am hungry for Your Word and Your presence. I pray that I will faithfully feast on Your message so that I may experience the fullness of Your Word and the benefit of its lasting nourishment.*

# Natural and Normal

～•～

*H*ave you ever lifted up a prayer with the sincere hope that God has a great sense of humor? Sometimes it isn't easy to put thoughts, needs, praises, and hopes into words, but God knows and understands you. You may think you're praying badly, but no prayer is ever done poorly in God's view. Your heavenly Father is perfectly kind and patient. He loves it when you go to Him with your prayers, no matter how lacking they may seem.

Pray regularly, and like anything else done faithfully and regularly, prayer will become more natural and normal for you. You're one of God's children, so talk to Him as a child who respects and honors a father. Acknowledge Him as your sustainer, provider, and guide. Psalm 23:3 promises, "He restores my soul; He leads me in the paths of righteousness." Let your words, whatever they are, lead you to the restorer of your soul—He'll lead from there.

*Lord, thank You for taking in my words and times of silence or tears. As my heavenly Father, You are eager to hear Your daughter. You delight in my efforts to be with You.*

# To All Generations

*As* time marches on, you'll want your life to leave a legacy for others. Let me encourage you today with the words of Psalm 33:11: "The counsel of the LORD stands forever, the plans of His heart to all generations." What better source of wisdom is there than the counsel of the Lord? What better confidence can you have than knowing God's wisdom is sufficient and enduring through every stage and age of your life? And what better legacy can you leave behind than to pass on God's eternal wisdom to the next generation of women through discipleship? Continue to grow spiritually, and you'll be a source of great strength and hope for everyone God brings across your path.

Seek a heart of wisdom, and then find a way to share from that heart.

*God, lead me to an ever-deepening faith and understanding of You. What a richness that will bring to my life and to the lives of younger Christian women I can encourage, teach, and mentor! Give me a heart to share my heart for You.*

# Priorities Change

*I* had such great plans for this time in my life. What happened?" Life can follow a lot of tangents when your priorities get out of whack. Ask yourself: What needs to be eliminated from my life that is not a priority?

Life has its seasons, and things change. Priorities change. What is God's plan for you now? Don't hold on to old self-made plans if God is asking you to move forward into a new purpose. If what you're doing doesn't promote that purpose or plan, eliminate it. I know it can be difficult to clean house when your life *is* that house. But you will feel lighter, more focused, and more content when you eliminate things that can get in the way between you and God and you and your purpose.

*Father, I want to let go of anything that has become unessential. Help me understand my priorities for this time of my life. I want every moment to be spent on activities, disciplines, and pursuits that lead to the path You have shaped for me.*

# A Valuable Model

~·~

*A*ctions speak louder than words. And children see us and our loud-and-clear declarations when others don't. They're quick to pick up on our conduct. Trust me—they're not going to listen to you preach something you don't practice. It's up to you to live out genuine faith before your children and other young Christians. That will give you credibility and a platform for teaching God's Word. And it will give your children a valuable model of a person who loves God and follows Him and His ways. Ephesians 6:4 says, "Do not exasperate your children; instead, bring them up in the training and instruction of the Lord" (NIV).

May this be true of you, my friend.

*Lord, I want to model godly behavior to my children. Give me insight into their needs so that I can be prayerful and wise as I provide godly counsel. I want to be encouraging as I instruct them in Your ways.*

# To the Glory of God

*H*ave you discovered the most effective diet? It's actually a *truth*. As a Christian woman you're not to be mastered by anything, including food. God's strength is far more powerful than any temptation. First Corinthians 10:31 says, "Whether you eat or drink, or whatever you do, do all to the glory of God." Even the most common acts of eating and drinking can be done in a way that honors our Lord.

For example, I'm in a five-step program that works for me and might be an encouragement to you in your effort to give this area of your life to God: (1) Don't eat too much. (2) Do eat only what is sufficient. (3) Eat only what you need. (4) Don't be mastered by anything. (5) Eat in a way that glorifies God. Remember, habit is overcome by *habit*. Be encouraged to do your best for God's best.

*God, I've given in to habits that stem more from boredom than hunger. I try to let food replace the void I feel when I'm lonely, angry, sad, or disappointed. You call me to Your presence, and You will fill that void in ways that food never can.*

# Your Days Are Numbered

~·~

"I'd love to do a missions trip—it's something to look forward to when I retire!" What is stopping you today from following through with godly longings? Your days are numbered, and only God knows how many you have left. Because there are no guarantees, it is important to depend on God's leading. Seize each and every day. Put the most into each moment and effort, and get the most out of it. The most joy. The most faith. And the most inspiration.

There are plenty of ways to do this. Love your family, help as many people as you can, give as much as you can. Pray daily for God to show you how to use your time and abilities. That's what the wise person does. When you grasp that you were made by God and for God, and that God has a purpose for your life, you live each moment for the Lord. A new energy, a new direction, and a new diligence will be given to you.

*Jesus, show me the way. I've asked before, but I feel really ready to embrace Your direction. Give me the energy and commitment to follow through. My numbered days matter not just to me and my family but to Your kingdom. Show me the way.*

# Pray—God's Way

*H*ave you ever thought, *God has forgotten me?* Life can be sobering and difficult. The Christian's life is no exception. James 1:2-4 says, "Count it all joy when you fall into various trials, knowing that the testing of your faith produces patience. But let patience have its perfect work, that you may be perfect and complete, lacking nothing." Note that James doesn't say *if* you have trials, but *when.* Trouble is inevitable. But when you face life with your eyes wide open, you'll discover a plan for handling trouble God's way.

Read and memorize Scripture verses that will help you through times of loss or uncertainty. Pray about the troubles of life and seek God's comfort and guidance. Your hope is in God, so when you're in trouble, pray. When you're feeling helpless, pray. God has not forgotten you. Stand back and wait to see the goodness of the Lord.

*Lord, I know that You are here with me. Your presence soothes my worries and smoothes the rough road. I will count it all joy to face this trial with Your strength and light.*

# Restore That One

~•~

*F*orgiveness and restoration are gifts we receive from God and extend to others. Galatians 6:1 reads, "If someone is caught in a sin, you who live by the Spirit should restore that person gently. But watch yourselves, or you also may be tempted" (NIV).

When a friend or family member is sinning, extend grace and encouragement. A forgiving heart is a heart that can pray for others, even for those who have hurt you. Pray for those you love, and for those who don't love you. Also, be aware of your own behavior. Turn the spotlight on your own actions and thoughts so that you will not be tempted to sin.

*God, You know the person who is in need of grace right now. Give me an eagerness to forgive. Help me release my hurt to Your care so I can pray without hesitation and with a pure heart.*

# When You Hurt

*I* thought we'd grow old together. Where did I miss the signals? What did I do?"

You may be this hurting person today. You may be crying out with those words of Scripture, "Has God forgotten to be gracious? Has He in anger shut up His tender mercies?" (Psalm 77:9). Not one day goes by that I don't receive a letter or an email from a woman who has been hurt in many ways by others.

I know firsthand that people hurt people. And even *God's* people hurt people. Family members hurt family members. The list goes on. When you wrestle with despair, when everything seems hopeless, put your God-given faith to work and trust in the Lord. Believe this! In whatever burden you bear, God will sustain you today and all the days of your life.

*Father, my tears keep flowing. I struggle to find the right words to pray. Hold me, Lord. I trust You and Your goodness.*

# God Keeps His Promise

*H*as someone in your past or present under-mined your trust? Broken promises can destroy your ability to trust for a long time. A promise is serious business—it is a vow, a pledge. The power of that promise depends on the integrity of the one making the promise. That means you can trust in God's promises.

Titus 1:2 describes our heavenly Father as the God who cannot lie. It doesn't get more reassuring than that. When you read a promise in the Bible, accept it with full confidence that God will do His part to fulfill that promise. It's His nature to do so. And God even promises to give you the resources you need to do your part. What a deal!

*God, Your faithfulness buoys my hope. Give me the integrity and character to keep my word to others and to You. I walk along my life path with confidence in Your promises and with deep gratitude for Your unfailing love.*

# Lay Aside All Malice

~•~

$\mathcal{A}$s the old proverb says, "Let not your tongue cut your throat." Gossip can never be taken back. It may seem harmless in the moment it is spoken, but it is never harmless. Your character and the character of the person you're talking about is compromised. And you dishonor God. No matter how much you apologize or try to make it right with someone you've discredited, the harm and hurt remain.

You are called by God to minister and to serve and to assist and to help—and to better the lives of others. And certainly, no life has ever been improved by gossip. First Peter 2:1 says you're to lay aside all malice and all evil speaking. Show your love for God by loving others.

*Lord, help me guard my tongue. Keep me from harmful words that discredit others and dishonor You. Give me a servant's heart that is gracious and humble.*

# A Disciplined Life

~•~

*I*magine having a more peaceful lifestyle. I don't know one woman whose stress and stressful situations don't cause her to wish for a simpler, calmer life. What I'm asking you to consider today is to stir up your passion for godliness. Aim to live with restraint, composure, and clarity. This isn't a mundane, boring life. Instead, it is a disciplined and focused life. In this day and age, personal discipline isn't exactly a popular goal. Maybe you think it'll limit your life experience, but it actually frees it.

My friend, this is what God desires of you and for you. This is what He wills for your life. This is the maturity He has in mind for you and me as women. Trade a life of wishes for a life of passion.

*God, as I grow in my faith, I realize that walking in Your purpose with faithful steps is exciting. You reveal new possibilities and give me the guidance and hope to move in them. This life is anything but boring!*

# Someone Who's Been There

~•~

Has a young person discovered your listening ear and kept you on speed-dial? Before you silence your phone, remember that encouraging younger women is one of God's high callings on your life. Teaching and encouraging someone who is younger is a privilege.

So many young women are desperate for an understanding friend, for someone who's "been there." When you show a young woman God's Word and then hold her accountable, it becomes a life-changing time of ministry for both of you. Assist her in living her life firmly rooted in God's Word. No matter what age you are, there is a woman younger than you who is longing for a connection with a godly mentor. Embrace the chance to serve in this way—you'll be so glad you did.

*Lord, guide me to a young woman who is ready for discipleship. I'm grateful for the women who have encouraged me with spiritual guidance over the years. I pray to serve in this way with great joy and with a heart inspired by gratitude.*

# 117
## What Are Your Children Learning?

*H*ave you had the uncomfortable experience of hearing something shocking come out of your children's mouths? When they talk back—or worse—your warning bell should sound off. Children need to learn to respect authority. And your teaching and reinforcement of this lesson is vital. You must hold your children accountable to following what the Bible teaches, which includes obeying their father, their mother, and their teacher. Train your children to have a godly attitude. When they understand kindness and compassion, they'll have a better understanding of respect. If you have little ones, God's calling isn't optional. They need to know who Jesus is and that He died for their sin. It is your privilege as a parent to point your child toward God and His Word. Take every opportunity to talk *about* God and *to* God with your children.

*Father, show me how to lead my children to a deep respect for You and others. Let my actions and words model humility and compassion. And let my conversations be filled with talk of Jesus so my children always know who has authority over my life and heart.*

# Caring for the Home

~•~

*D*oes the word *homemaker* make you think of the 1950s instead of your multitasking, contemporary existence today? Old-fashioned or not, making a home is God's high calling. Contrary to current thinking, it isn't a prison with a life sentence. A home is not a place where you're "kept." Caring for the home and providing a safe haven for the people you love is such a joy. And because it's God's high calling for you, why not make it a passion?

My personal philosophy is, "If there's anything I must do or have to do, I try to do it with passion." Try to give your homemaking responsibilities your absolute best. Your all. Shouldn't your work be done willingly and passionately? There is not a more rewarding labor of love than making a home centered on God.

*God, forgive me for grumbling about my responsibilities at home. I want to create a place of peace, welcome, and godliness for all who dwell there. Give me a great passion for my home and my family.*

# Temper the Temper

~·~

*T*hrowing an adult temper tantrum is never good. If your behavior has included sulking, yelling, or giving your husband or a friend the silent treatment, then you've officially embraced the behavior of a toddler. Childishness has no place in the life of a woman of God. It's time to grow up. You might experience some growing pains, because it does take work. I still have moments when I want to give in to selfish behaviors, but thankfully those times have become rarer.

Wisdom is essential for the woman of God. Ask the Lord to help you trim out the meaningless and secondary things in life. Wisdom is choosing the best of the best for your minutes and your strength. It means choosing to live according to God's priorities. By God's grace, make *His* best choice for you today in *your* choice of actions, words, and responses.

*Lord, may all my behaviors reflect my desire to grow in Your wisdom. When I feel the old behaviors rise up, give me the self-control to resist them. I have Your Word to steady my reactions and emotions. Help me grow into a lovely woman of God.*

# Praying in Friendship

*⌒•⌒*

"Lunch with Brenda next Tuesday. Call Maria on Thursday. Friday, get an email off to Deb." I've never liked the term *social butterfly,* and believe me, that's not me. But I do like my prayer life to be social—one that includes an expanse of friends and acquaintances. Every week I write down the names of several dear friends. Then I try to call or communicate with each of them in some way. Isn't email great? I also regret that many a week flies by without the much-desired contact. But at least I'm trying.

Who do you want to commit to prayer for this week? And who might need a letter, an email, or a phone call for encouragement? Finding out about another woman's particular concerns will help you pray more specifically and more intimately for her. It's all about balance and being a woman of commitment.

*Lord, today I pray specifically for my dearest friends. Give me an attentiveness and awareness so my prayers are in line with Your will for them and with their hurts and hopes. When life gets too busy, Lord, please bring to mind a friend or acquaintance needing the comfort of prayer.*

# A Decision's Seven Steps

~·~

Do you want to be let in on a great way to make decisions? Here it is in seven steps: Stop, wait, pray, search the Scriptures, ask for wise counsel, make a decision, and create a plan.

I cannot begin to tell you how valuable these seven steps have been to me over the years. They've saved me from sinning, from making foolish choices—for the smallest decisions right on up the scale to the earth-shattering, life-changing ones. James 3:17 says, "The wisdom that is from above is first pure, then peaceable, gentle, willing to yield, full of mercy and good fruits, without partiality and without hypocrisy." Read through those steps again with a particular decision in mind. Don't be afraid to wait in prayer. God will give you the wisdom that is His.

> *God, guide me toward right and righteous decisions. I'm excited to move toward action and plans in ways that are pleasing to You. And when You ask me to wait, I'll do so with anticipation and peace in the presence of Your love.*

# A Fervent Heart

~·~

*A* call once in a while, a lunch date, dinner. What's the harm?" No harm at all, my friend, if you're talking about getting together for lunch with your *girl* friend. Proverbs 2:17 makes it clear than an adulterous wife and woman is described as one who has forgotten "the covenant of her God." Marriage vows are made before God and in His presence.

When the fervency of your heart for God slips from hot to lukewarm or cold, your actions and choices will reflect the temperature change. They will reflect the condition of your heart. Pray for a heart that is passionate about purity. It's one of your highest callings as a woman. Reverent and holy behavior preserves the integrity of your foundation of faith—and will give you the strength to remain true to your covenant.

*Faithful God, my vows made before You are my cherished reminder to serve my marriage, husband, and my commitment to You with great reverence and care. Give me Your discernment so that I never allow my faith to turn lukewarm and passionless.*

# Good and Kind

In our "every person for themselves" culture, it's easy to underestimate the importance of goodness and kindness. Gentleness, consideration, and sympathy are qualities that every woman of God should cultivate. I pray those are character traits my children will ascribe to me. Are you known for your kindness? Gentleness? For being a beautiful-on-the-inside woman? Kindness is love in action in the little things. Things that seem scarcely worth doing and yet mean a great deal to those receiving generosity or hospitality. Kindness is a cheerful word when someone's discouraged. Someone has said that kindness goes about performing little ministries with a touch of blessing.

My prayer is the one prayed by Saint Francis of Assisi: "Lord, grant that I may seek rather to comfort, than to be comforted; to understand, than to be understood; to love, than to be loved."

*Heavenly Father, help me put aside my plans, my agenda, my to-do list so I am fully aware of how I might extend gentleness, goodness, and kindness to others. Show me what it means to love as Your Son loved.*

# Be of Good Cheer

*I*'m done. This is just too much. I can't believe this is God's plan for my life!" This is not an uncommon confession among Christian women. I wish I could tell you differently, but suffering is part of this life. Every one of us will face times of trial and loss. But let me encourage you with Jesus' words in John 16:33: "These things I have spoken to you, that in Me you may have peace. In the world you will have tribulation; but be of good cheer, I have overcome the world." Jesus doesn't promise you the easy life when you choose to follow Him. But in times of suffering you can experience His peace and a great joy.

If you are disheartened today, look to the Lord for your peace and joy. Rejoice in the truth that He has overcome the world and its brokenness, and look to the future glory He promises His suffering children. These are promises for you.

*Lord, You see my suffering right now, and You've seen so much suffering since the beginning of creation. But You have overcome the world, and in Your strength I will persevere and overcome. I will be of good cheer and great hope because You are my Lord.*

# Sincere Love

~•~

You've probably heard it preached a hundred times, but putting the command to "love one another" into action is not ordinary, it is extraordinary. This call to you as a woman who belongs to God is to go one step further: You're to love others in deed and in truth. Sincere love doesn't pretend. It has no ulterior motives; it wants nothing from the one loved. Is there any person in your life who's not receiving your sincere love? God is calling you to a love that costs greatly and requires effort. It's easy to talk about how much you love God, but loving others reveals how much you truly love God. How are you measuring up? Are there any changes you plan to make in the sincerity of how you love?

*God, help me love the person who is difficult to love. Remove any judgments or past disappointments that keep me from offering sincere love to certain people in my life. I want to love with Your love. Guide me in this pursuit of godly character.*

# *Bible Study Is Life-changing*

～•～

*A*re you ready for a life makeover? A real one that transforms you from the inside out? If that's your desire, I highly recommend you begin studying your Bible! Follow those in Acts 17:11 who "searched the Scriptures daily." It's the only way to grow in Christ.

One of the noblest pursuits a child of God can undertake is to get to know and understand God better. And the best way to accomplish that is to look carefully at the book God has written—the Bible. For example, when you read a passage of Scripture, ask yourself a few helpful questions: How does the truth revealed in the passage affect my relationship with God? My relationships with others? How does this truth affect the way I live?

Don't merely answer the questions. Put into practice what God teaches you in your study. When you do, God will bless your efforts.

*God, You are all-knowing and all-powerful. I trust You to lead me. First, I must seek You and Your Word so I am quick to walk in Your ways.*

# Precious Time

~·~

*A*re you right in the middle of a hectic moment? Great! It's the perfect time to take a break.

Yes, I'm serious. As crazy as it may sound, take time right now to wait on the Lord in prayer. Martin Luther said, "Prayer is the most important thing in my life. If I should neglect prayer for a single day, I would lose a great deal of the fire of my faith."

Pretty powerful words! To keep the fire of your faith alive, you must realize that *every*thing hinges on your offering of precious, hard-to-come-by, limited time. Your best work and good deeds and, yes, your hectic schedule all depend on the sacrificial gift to God of your *time*. Rely on His strength and power for all that you do.

*Lord, I am taking a prayer break right now. Time with You and in stillness waiting on Your leading is my path to a passionate faith. When I wake up in the morning, let my first act be to offer my day up to You as my sacrifice.*

# Speaking of Jesus

~•~

*D*o you share your faith with others, or do you hold back from talking about God and what He is doing in your life? I encourage you to earnestly pray for opportunities to introduce your friends to Christ. There's no greater gift you could give to them. Paul prayed in Colossians 4:3 that God would open a door "to speak the mystery of Christ." To walk in wisdom toward non-Christians. That he would make the most of every opportunity.

As you form friendships with neighbors, co-workers, and friends, let them see Christ through your love. There should never be any doubt about your relationship with God through Christ. Make Paul's prayer your own with his encouragement to "let your speech always be with grace, seasoned with salt, that you may know how you ought to answer each one" (verse 6). Reach out—and speak out!

*Lord, fill my speech with sincere talk of my faith and Your love. Don't let me hold back out of fear or shyness. I want others to know the hope they can have in You. Nudge me, Lord. Show me who to reach out to this week.*

# Motivation Is Key

*W*hat motivates you? Is there anything that gives you a burst of energy and diligence? It's good to evaluate where your passions lie. For me, motivation is key to everything I do. I'm constantly thinking and praying about what I want for my life, my marriage, my family. I seek God's leading about how to contribute to my church, to God's people. I want to have God as the driving force behind all I do.

When your faith is the spark of motivation and inspiration for all areas of your life, you'll experience a longing to know what God is asking of you. And when you want something badly enough, it spurs you to do the work to make it happen. How has God been moving in your life recently? Recognize this, and be moved to action. He will give you the strength of mind and spirit to run toward your purpose with great motivation and commitment.

*Lord, I am motivated to live out my faith. To express my gratitude to my giving God. To seek fulfillment in Your purposes for me. Give me a heart that is motivated by a longing to serve You in everything I do.*

# Get Involved

~·~

*I*'d like to do something significant. I'm just not sure what it should be." Ask God how you can extend your hands and be involved in His work. Roll up your sleeves and prepare to experience amazing opportunities.

The women mentioned in Luke chapter 8 followed Jesus and supported Him financially. What an incredible, noble example for you and me. You can do likewise by encouraging the ministries of individuals and organizations with your gifts and support. You can contribute to a Christian charity or commit to sponsoring a missionary family you know. Consider assisting a Bible or seminary student by giving to scholarship funds. Help a college student by praying for them and providing them with a home-cooked meal and family time. Support young people who are going on a missions trip. Ask God where He wants you to be involved.

*God, how can I support a ministry or a person today? Where and how should I help? I love that Jesus' ministry was supported by women. Give me the same desire those women had. What a joy and honor it is to participate in the work of the Lord!*

# Less Is Best

~·~

*H*ave you ever said more than you intended? We've all been there, haven't we? When it comes to words, less is almost always best. Then you're less likely to speak out of turn or in a way that hurts people or isn't pleasing to God. Proverbs 10:19 reminds us that "sin is not ended by multiplying words, but the prudent hold their tongues" (NIV). Another proverb points out that even a fool is counted wise when he holds his peace. It's better to be quiet and be thought a fool than to speak and remove all doubt. If you've ever gone too far in trying to explain and justify your actions, you know just what this proverb means! But when you follow God's standards for your life, your speech will be beautiful. My prayer is that God will grow you into a woman who "opens her mouth with wisdom, and on her tongue is the law of kindness" (Proverbs 31:26).

> *Lord, save me from myself and my own tongue. I get into trouble when I speak too much and pray too little. Give me patience, kindness, and respect so that when I do speak, my words are filled with Your wisdom.*

# Your Sacrifice of Praise

~•~

*I*s there a woman you know who makes everyone feel better when she's around? Is that what people think about you, my friend? Consider how you can be a more joyful person. When you are a woman who offers praise to God, you'll transform your pain into joy. You'll also be quick to encourage others with godly wisdom and kindness. Learn to give thanks in the good and in the bad. Thank God for His perfect timing, His perfect plan, and His unconditional love. Hebrews 13:15 says, "Let us continually offer the sacrifice of praise to God…giving thanks to His name."

Focus on the reality of God's promises. Take your focus off your suffering and turn your eyes to Jesus. And obey God's command to be joyful always. Don't sit around waiting for your circumstance to make you joyful. Go to God to be filled with His joy.

*Lord, let praises fall from my lips out of the fullness of my gratitude and joy. I will turn my focus from my troubles to Your face for reassurance and leading. From this place of peace, lead me to be a woman who makes others know Your joy.*

# Practice Kindness

~·~

"I'm more than happy to help out—just let me know when you need something." Expressing this to a friend is one way to be available. But wouldn't it be so much kinder to notice a person's needs and not wait to be asked?

The Bible says in Proverbs 20:12, "The hearing ear and the seeing eye, the LORD has made them both." Care for people in the same way God cares for you—with an attentive heart. Be on the lookout for ways to serve. When you begin to notice others, it doesn't take long to know their wants and needs. Constantly ask God to help you care, to notice, and to touch the people He places in your life. Developing the practice of kindness is a part of the joy and wonder of walking with God daily.

*God, guide me to be generous with my help. Give me a perceptive heart so I am able to come to the aid of others with prayers, resources, wisdom, and comfort. You provide for me in so many ways. Show me how to model Your heart of abundance.*

# That Problem Person

~·~

*A*re you ready to put your prayer life to the test? It may be difficult for you to do, but I'm going to ask you to choose your number one problem person, and take him or her before the Lord in prayer. Then go a step further and ask God to help you show His kindness to the very person who hurt you, caused your pain, or may be making your life miserable.

Luke 6:28 says, "Bless those who curse you, and pray for those who spitefully use you." You'll find you cannot hate a person you're praying for. Try it. The Bible says love suffers patiently and is kind. Pray for God to fill your heart with His compassion as you walk each day—and every step along the way with Him.

*God, give me a heart for the one who troubles me, who pushes my buttons. I want to have Your view of that person, Your love for him or her. Release me from my negative attitude and preconceived notions so that I move forward with kindness, grace, and a vulnerable heart.*

# God Is Faithful

~•~

From the opening page of the Bible to the last last, you will see God's faithfulness. I'm always moved by the words of Psalm 89:1: "I will sing of the mercies of the LORD forever; with my mouth will I make known Your faithfulness to all generations." When you know God's faithfulness, you receive courage. You can endure your trials because you're certain you can count on Him. I know you've had experiences with people who've failed you, disappointed you, or hurt you. Some people may have even mistreated you. But God will not let you down. And as Scripture says of itself in Revelation 22:6, "These words are faithful and true." We are indeed a blessed people to be eternally experiencing the faithfulness of God.

*Lord, I do want to sing of Your mercies forever. In times of trouble or doubt, I don't question Your presence. You bring healing to my wounds caused by the unfaithfulness of others. And You restore my faith in a future and a hope.*

# With Gusto

~•~

"Reading? Nothing interests me. Bible study? Too much memorizing. Friends? Why bother?" Have you ever had a season—and maybe it's right now—when you've had no zest for life? Being tired is a physical challenge. But being lazy? That's an entirely different issue! Laziness says, "I don't want to do it." But God's Word says to change your focus and set your mind on things above. Second Corinthians 4:18 says, "We fix our eyes not on what is seen, but on what is unseen, since what is seen is temporary, but what is unseen is eternal" (NIV). In other words, get your eyes off of yourself and the world's temporary stuff and look straight into the face of Jesus. Give matters of the eternity and the heart utmost importance *and* effort. Whatever you do, do it for the Lord—and do it with gusto.

*Father, I'm sorry for the times I've been lazy about matters of eternal importance. I have let the pursuit of tangible possessions or concrete results rule my day. No wonder I am tired. Fill me with Your strength and priorities. I want to serve You with vitality and conviction.*

# Be of Good Courage

*D*oes today look a lot like yesterday? I understand how discouraging that can be. If you hunger for more life, more living, and more variety, go straight to God.

You need His encouragement and guidance as you press on in the tasks He has given to you. As a young mother of preschoolers, I struggled with this feeling of living the same day over and over. Dealing with children is so constant, so draining, so demanding. And there were many days when I didn't see any progress, any hope. It's times like this when you want to give up or you question the value of even trying. Fear sets in, and you become afraid of failing. But then you are given reassurance in Joshua 1:9: "Be strong and of good courage; do not be afraid, nor be dismayed, for the LORD your God is with you wherever you go." God is faithful, dear friend—He is a God of hope!

*Faithful Lord, You are with me now. You ease my fears and You show me that each day does matter. I want the courage to embrace each day as a gift and to use it for Your glory. Your presence restores my hope, and this hope renews my heart.*

# God's Assertiveness

*If* you're wondering if you can be aggressive to push for your rights, your claim to status, or your "deserved" fruits of labor, it's good to look to Psalm 46:10, which says, "Be still, and know that I am God." The real meaning of this verse may just surprise you. The Hebrew word translated "be still" actually means "stop striving." This puts a different spin on it, doesn't it? God is telling us, "Stop it. Stop all your struggling. I, God, will do this."

We're to let go of our rights, our posturing, and our strategies and leave the unfolding of purpose in God's sovereign hand. The result is a gentle spirit. And gentleness is the opposite of self-assertiveness and self-interest. Does it mean you're to be a doormat for others to walk over? No, it's the evidence of a powerful and loving God at work in your life.

*Lord, keep me from striving. I find myself struggling and becoming hardhearted as I push in my own power. Help me lean into Your gentle, mighty strength and follow Your will in stillness and with total reliance on You.*

# Don't Do It

*As* a child of God, "Don't do it" means just that. When temptation comes your way, you're to call on God for His strength, and then—don't do it! In other words, don't give in to emotions, to cravings, to urges. Don't think or do what you know is against God's Word. Don't make the easy choices when God is calling you to press on. Don't rationalize sinful behaviors and harmful words and actions. When the Bible speaks of "self-control," it means the ability to say no. It's an evidence of willpower that sometimes expresses itself in "won't power."

In what ways and for what behaviors do you need "won't power" right now? Call on God and trust His power to help you persevere through a temptation. Galatians 5 says the fruit of the Spirit is…self-control! Live in the Spirit, my friend.

*God, grant me Your "won't power" today. I need it. I've been justifying the same behavior for a long time now and it is hurting me, my walk with You, and others in my life who depend on me to be a woman of honor and integrity. I need Your strength, God.*

# God's Strength

*A* broken heart really is painful. But where there is a broken heart, there is also God's mending and healing. When everything seems at its worse, God will bring hope. My friend, God is faithful. Jeremiah 29:11 promises, "'For I know the plans I have for you,' declares the LORD, 'plans to prosper you and not to harm you, plans to give you hope and a future'" (NIV).

And one of more than 8000 promises in the Bible says you can do all things through Christ because He strengthens you. The loss of that boyfriend, the child who has strayed from God, the career that isn't going as you planned—your lack of hope can never wipe out God's goodness. Rejoice in Psalm 100:5: "Weeping may endure for a night, but joy comes in the morning."

*Lord, You ease my pain, You take the sting from my heartache, and You bring joy with the new dawn. I trust in Your ways and Your promises, my dear Lord.*

# Enduring Love

~•~

*D*o you have an ongoing burden? My heart goes out to you as each new day brings with it a hardship that must be endured. Trust in the Lord today, and again tomorrow. Live in God's constant and powerful presence no matter what you're required to do or asked to give up.

When you feel solitary in your daily trial, know that you're *never* alone. Deuteronomy 33:27 says, "The eternal God is your refuge, and underneath are the everlasting arms." Isn't it such a comfort to know that your life, with its ongoing struggles, is carried by the Lord? You can give Him the weight of every worry. Philippians 4:7 says, "The peace of God, which surpasses all understanding, will guard your hearts and minds through Christ Jesus." Wait patiently for the Lord. He hears your cries, and He extends to you an enduring love.

*Father, You know what I face each day. Give me peace in my circumstances. Grant me patience when my heart is restless. And guide me with the light of hope through this journey.*

# I Did It My Way

*I* try as hard as I can, but I blow it every time." If you're frustrated by some recent mistakes, don't be discouraged. The first 30 years of my life, I made a lot of errors. I wanted happiness, fulfillment, and a life of meaning on my terms. I wanted to make sure that my life counted. And thrown into the mix was a marriage that was going from bad to worse.

It wasn't until we became a Christian family that things began to change. It was a miracle of God's grace. Whether you're married or single, the answer is the same—God first. Second Peter 3:18 says, "Grow in the grace and knowledge of our Lord and Savior Jesus Christ." Time in prayer and time in God's Word come first.

*God, how did I end up here again? Forgive me for trying to do things on my own and for my own purposes. I give my life over to Your leading. I want to grow in the grace and knowledge of the Lord and have that maturity be evident in my life.*

# Team Players

~·~

*A*re you one of those wives with a "when-then" attitude? *When* he does this or that—*then* I'll do this or that. It undoubtedly works, but to what end? Your assignment from God is not to change your husband, but to love, follow, assist, and minister to him. So before you get too critical, check your own motives. If you tear him down, is it so you feel better about yourself?

Ecclesiastes 4:9 says, "Two are better than one, because they have a good reward for their labor." The goal is to work together as a *team*. I guarantee you it will make a difference in your marriage. There's no substitute for the strength that blesses a couple when they work together.

*God, show me how to encourage my husband. I don't want to hold back from being a help to him. Guide me toward a grateful and generous heart.*

# Make a Difference

*D*id you wake up and say, "Oh no, another day of *this* marriage!" If that's you today, what are you going to do about it? If you're bored, let the light of inspiration shine on your life. Little things can make a big difference. Let your admiration shine for all to see—especially your husband. Do you tell him to do things instead of asking him? Do you need to stop putting him down in front of others? It wouldn't hurt to keep a list of ways to show respect as a reminder—in case you slip up. It happens.

Titus 2:4 says to love your husband—to be kind to him. Think about what kind of meal he might enjoy. Plan a Saturday filled with activities he likes. Be willing to let God make a difference through you. Set up a time to be together and make a difference in both of your lives.

*Lord, give me hope and inspiration to be a light in my marriage. I long to make a difference in the world, yet I neglect to make a difference in the most important relationship in my life. Show me how to invest joy in my marriage.*

# Cut It Out

~•~

*A*s women of God who desire to be wives after God's own heart, we must keep our speech patterns pure and right and anger-free. James 1:20 tells us that "human anger does not produce the righteousness that God desires" (NIV). Our wrong, unproductive words do not accomplish the will or purposes of God.

Basically, if you're speaking out of anger and frustration, cut it out. If you're struggling in this area, ask God for help. Your communication with your husband—or anyone, for that matter—will improve a thousand percent when you stop using venomous words.

Clear your heart and speech of unkindness, jealousy, sarcasm, or indifference. You'll be glad you did. And I guarantee your husband will too.

*Jesus, keep my heart and intentions pure. I don't want to weigh down my relationship with anger. Help me cut out the hurtful talk so I can add in words of hope and praise.*

# Serious Business

~·~

*P*raying to God is a reward and a blessing. But it's also serious business. You have to decide to make prayer a priority. Then there's the challenge of making the time in your busy schedule. And it's best to arrange for a place in your home where it's quiet and calm. That's not always easy!

I want my heart to be like that of King David in the psalms: "As the deer pants for the water brooks, so pants my soul for You, O God" (Psalm 42:1).

Imagine the transformation that would take place in your heart if you spent more time each day drawing near to God through His Word and prayer. To long for God is to be guided by your heart to the source of all life. What could be more important than that?

*God, I want to be in Your presence. Help me be strong in my commitment to meet with You each day. Being with You is a serious pursuit…and a serious blessing, Lord.*

# Godly Wisdom

*I*s there someone in your life who drains your energy? Whose problems consume you? You must meet Abigail. She was married to an alcoholic tyrant named Nabal. His very name meant "fool." You can imagine the tightrope she walked. Yet Abigail was applauded in 1 Samuel 25 for her dazzling wisdom, when she stopped a potential bloodbath between her foolish husband and the avenging warrior David and his 400 troops.

Abigail could see the big picture. She kept her composure under pressure. She formed a plan. She spoke with wisdom. And she effectively influenced others. Every challenge or responsibility that lies before you can be handled in a godly way.

*Lord, give me wisdom that reveals what needs to be done for Your purposes. When I'm intimidated about standing strong in my faith, remind me to let You work through me. I want to be a woman of godly influence.*

# Top Priority

~·~

*T*o make a goal or objective a priority, you must put passion behind it. Mark 12:30 says, "You shall love the Lord your God with all your heart, with all your soul, with all your mind, and with all your strength." This is the first commandment, and it is the way of a passionate faith.

Make God a priority by increasing your love for and knowledge of His Word. Read it each day to draw near to His heart. I want God to be first in my life—so why not put Him first in my day? Before the day gets going and before everyone else is up, fill your mind with God's Word.

*God, each moment that I spend immersed in Your Word is a moment that I feel embraced by Your loving arms. The longer I train my thoughts on You, the more completely I want to give You my heart, my soul, my mind, and my strength.*

# Take Care of Yourself

~·~

*I*f I feel this bad now, what will I feel like when I'm older?" Have you noticed that there is a cause and effect to your troubles? When you fail to exercise, your body becomes weaker or has problems, then exercise can become more difficult to do. When you don't watch what you eat, you feel uncomfortable in your clothes and in your own skin. When you aren't sleeping well, your energy level is low, or you have high blood pressure. Those days when you watch TV or stay on the Internet until all hours, you end up feeling lifeless and even farther from your goals.

You're getting the picture—there's a difference between selfishness and taking care of yourself. I want you to be around to live out God's priority for your life. First Timothy 4:7 says, "Exercise yourself toward godliness." Begin by taking care of yourself.

*Lord, give me the desire to be well, to be fit, to be physically strong so that I am able to serve You and my family with greater energy. I want to be able to walk—no, run!—toward the purpose You have for me.*

# Follow a Plan

~·~

*J*ust for tomorrow, follow a plan! And be prepared to say *no* to your usual excuses for avoiding a schedule or plan of action. This will be your day to make it happen by relying on God's help. You can do it! Set your alarm clock for 30 minutes earlier than usual. And get up when the buzzer sounds. Read your Bible and pray during that extra time. You'll be off to a great start, my friend.

Put some order in your day. Do those acts of love you planned so others can know you consider them a priority. And take care of yourself—for just one day. Wow—what a day it'll be! Tuck Matthew 6:33 in your pocket and read it over and over: "Seek first the kingdom of God and His righteousness, and all these things shall be added to you."

*God, You want to add to my life, but I keep filling my time with meaningless or distracting activities. I will create breathing room in my day to listen for Your voice, and to follow the plan You have for me.*

# God's Truth

~·~

*T*he truth of God's Word can change a life—yours! Hebrews 4:12 says, "The word of God is living and powerful, and sharper than any two-edged sword, piercing even to the division of soul and spirit...and is a discerner of the thoughts and intents of the heart."

God's Word works on the inside. As you read the Bible, you'll begin to identify wrong behavior, use tools to mend your ways, and experience a change of perspective on your day. Psalm 19:8-10 says, "The statutes of the LORD are right, rejoicing the heart; the commandment of the LORD is pure, enlightening the eyes; the fear of the LORD is clean, enduring forever; the judgments of the LORD are true and righteous altogether. More to be desired are they than gold, yea, than much fine gold; sweeter also than honey and the honeycomb." Don't ever underestimate the value and the sweetness of God's instruction.

*Lord, use Your living Word to pierce my innermost being. Know my heart, my thoughts, and my intentions. Refine them to fit Your ways and to be in line with Your sweet and righteous truths.*

# A New Season

~·~

*I*'d really like to do something new, but I'd have to add another night to the week to make it happen." There is another answer. If you dropped something you're already doing, you can make some time.

As Solomon observed in Ecclesiastes 3:1, everything has a season. Maybe you're single. Next year you may be married. Or you may be in the season of child-raising. Or like me, in the season of doing all the things I set aside until my children were raised.

The point is, check what you're doing. And eliminate those things that aren't contributing to God's plan and priorities for you. It can be hard to pare away activities, but this act of obedience and faith will open your time and life up to all God wants you to focus on.

*Lord, grant me perspective that is in line with Your priorities. Give me a heart for this season I'm in so I can make the most of it and use it for Your glory.*

# *Labor of Love*

~•~

*T*idying your living room and cleaning your kitchen might not feel like doing God's work, but it is. Believe me, I'm very humbled that keeping up my home is a way I can bring honor and glory to God. I praise God that, in some small ways, I've learned to serve my husband and children.

It's a labor of love to create a refuge that is organized, comfortable, peaceful, and safe and secure. I can honestly say there's no blessing like that of a happy home.

First Corinthians 4:2 says it is required of a steward that he or she be found faithful. We are called to set aside self and do the work of building a home where love reigns and order prevails.

*I have to admit, Lord, that my attitude toward caring for my home has not been joyful. But I want to create a sanctuary for my family. And I want guests to feel the generosity of Your love and grace when they enter. Help me embrace this labor of love.*

# Overindulging in Ministry

~•~

*W*hen you are trying to model a servant's heart, it can be easy to lose sight of healthy and godly boundaries. If you're overindulging in ministry to others while everyone at home misses your presence and care, you need to reset your priorities. If you're neglecting your marriage, your family, your home, or your own physical health, you need to think again about how you're serving the Lord.

Are those family members happy with the attention, or *lack* of attention, they're receiving? Is your husband fully—and I mean *fully*—supportive of your involvement at church? You can have good intentions and still be off track from God's will for you and your family.

Few things are more rewarding for a Christian couple than serving the Lord together. Maybe not always together as in "side by side." But certainly "together" as in of one mind!

*Father, I want to be blessed with the focus and energy to use my gifts as You see fit. Guide my actions and guard my intentions so I move forward with my family as we serve You together.*

# Patience

~·~

Patience has never come easy for me either. Thankfully, God's Word is faithful to come to the rescue. Jesus' surefire method for patience was prayer. First Peter 2:23 says that Jesus kept entrusting Himself to God, who judges righteously.

Allow God to soothe your pain as you do nothing. Let Him fill you with His patience as you endure the hurt. God calls us to be patient with others.

How long can you wait? Well, make that period a little longer. How many times can you wait? Make it a few more times. Follow Jesus' example. No one ever endured more than Jesus did, and He trusted God and God's timing in all circumstances.

*God, my patience wears thin so quickly these days. Give me a faithful heart that waits on Your word to move forward, to be still, to keep praying. I entrust my life and my daily walk to Your guidance.*

# Think Kindness

～•～

*A*re you maturing as a woman of God? A sure sign of spiritual growth is when you begin to think about others. "Thinking" is a part of kindness. Consider what thoughts illuminate a kind heart: "What would help her? What does she need? How can I help?" When David became king of Israel he asked, "Is there still anyone who is left of the house of Saul, that I may show him kindness?" (2 Samuel 9:1).

David was thinking about showing kindness to the heirs of the former king. Can you think of someone you can be kind to? Ask God to give you a caring heart. Look around. See the needs of people in your home, your neighborhood, where you work. Hurting people are everywhere. Touch a life with kindness.

*Jesus, show me who needs to experience Your kindness, gentleness, and care today. Release me from any pride or reservations that would keep me from following Your leading. Help me reach the hurting with Your love, Lord.*

# Love Means Action

~·~

"How am I supposed to know she's having a rough time? I talk to her every week and she never mentioned it!" It's sad to find out someone in your life has been hurting and you didn't realize it. But these situations are a reminder to always pay attention to God's leading. When you feel God directing you to check in with a friend or ask how a co-worker is doing, do it. And then take the initiative to meet specific needs of others.

Love means action. And sometimes that requires forgetting about your comfort level or your preference to stay on the sidelines. I understand why that's a bit scary. It's risky to approach someone—even caringly. But do it.

Ask God to help you. He will. Give every goodness you can think of, even to those who've hurt you. Put kind thoughts into action. The goal is to grow in godliness, not just to crank out good works. Cultivate goodness—God's way.

*God, impress upon my heart the urgency of meeting the needs around me. Work within and through me so I cultivate a kind and generous spirit. How can I be Your hands today?*

# Be Faithful

~•~

*F*aithfulness is often thought of in terms of marriage and fidelity. But 1 Timothy 3:11 says to be "faithful in all things." Faithfulness is defined as loyalty, trustworthiness. It's characteristic of the person who's reliable. And as part of your walk with God, you will experience a deepening faithfulness to God and His will, to God and His Word, and to others.

Being faithful in word and deed requires commitment and obedience. When God called us to be faithful in all things, He made it a major distinction of a Christian woman. It's a quality He's given you to benefit the entire body of Christ. It's your time to respond. Seek to become more faithful in all things, in all ways.

*Lord, show me how to be obedient to Your call to faithfulness. May I honor You with my decisions and commitments. Show me what it means to truly be a faithful woman of God in all things.*

# Power Fruit

~·~

Gentleness and meekness? Were these the characteristics you thought you'd aim for as you grew in greater understanding of yourself and your abilities? Or do assertive and successful better describe your original plans for yourself?

Let's talk about that. My idea of a woman who is gentle and meek is that she can take it. She bears the disturbances others create. She endures ill treatment. She withstands misunderstandings. And she carries the image of Jesus and His suffering in her heart. She handles it with strength. I encourage you to open your heart and mind to gentleness. God so desires gentleness to characterize your life. In the eyes of the world today, gentleness may look like weakness. But in Galatians 5:23, God calls it the fruit of His Spirit. And producing that kind of fruit calls for the greatest of strength. It's the power fruit.

*Lord, help me let go of my old views of gentleness and meekness. I used to see these qualities as weak but now view them for what they are—characteristics of godly strength and quiet, enduring power.*

# A Fresh Start

*I* can't seem to let go of the past. What I did in those years still haunts me." God's love for you accomplished the forgiveness of your sin, your cleansing, your new birth, and your fresh start.

Remind yourself of the truth of 2 Corinthians 5:17: "If anyone is in Christ, he is a new creation; old things have passed away; behold, all things have become new."

Are you living as a new creation? Each day that you hold on to the weight of past mistakes and sins, you aren't living in the freedom of Christ. Old things have passed away. So the next time your past sin comes to mind, acknowledge God's forgiveness, thank Him, and move on to a life of hope and grace.

*Lord, thank You for Your grace. Give me the strength to walk in it. I want to fully experience life as Your new creation.*

# Four Life-changing Questions

*T*wo children and ten years of marriage later, and I'm wondering, *What was I thinking?*" You are wise to ask a question, but I have four questions that will better help you grasp God's purpose for your life: Who am I? Where did I come from? Why am I here? And where am I going? Don't answer these based on what others think or need or want from you. What do *you* think? God has a specific purpose for you, and your answers to these questions will be life-changing.

Ephesians 1:4 says, "Before he made the world, God loved us and chose us in Christ to be holy and without fault in his eyes. God decided in advance to adopt us into his own family by bringing us to himself through Jesus Christ. This is what he wanted to do, and it gave him great pleasure" (NLT). Let a clear understanding of your identity in Christ shed light on all the ways you can live out your purpose through your marriage, your parenting, and your daily walk with God.

> *You give me purpose, Lord. When I lose sight of what my life is about, help me embrace my identity as a part of Your family. And help me delight in the gift of life—every part of it!*

# Reach Forward

*A*re you content right where you are? If so, I'm not so sure that's a *good* thing! In Philippians 3:14 Paul wrote, "I press toward the goal for the prize of the upward call of God in Christ Jesus." His desire was to get out of his comfort zone so he could grow in his faith in Christ. How many times have you prayed for that? It's a difficult prayer because being comfortable and having a routine offer some sense of security. But it is a false security if God is pressing you to purposefully look ahead and reach forward. For that to occur, there's got to be some tension in life. Healthy tension.

Too much comfort invites you to *watch* the race rather than *participate* in it. Paul calls us to reach "forward to those things which are ahead" (Philippians 3:13). Press on and move on!

*Jesus, You call me forward so that I step from complacency to an active, vibrant faith. Thank You for leading the way. You are by my side as I look ahead and reach beyond my comfort zone to the prize of an upward call.*

# God Knows Every Step

Is life unfolding the way you thought it would? Does it seem like you're living your backup plan instead of your intended life? God knows. He allows and He plans every step. Romans 8:28 states it up front: "We know that all things work together for good to those who love God, to those who are the called according to His purpose." God has designed your life. He has a plan and is actively working out His will through the people, events, and circumstances around you—past, present, and future. There's never been a mistake. You will have hope when you acknowledge that God has planned your life and that His best purpose is being played out. God is the author of every moment of your life—*every* moment.

*God, all of my life has been written by You. When I worry about being "off schedule," I will take hold of Your hand. And You will continue to guide me toward the good, the calling, and the hope You have planned all along.*

# Trust God—Today

~•~

*A*re you giving all of your life to the Lord? Proverbs 16:3 gives you a command and a beautiful promise: "Commit your works to the LORD, and your thoughts will be established." Start right now and commit today to God. I guarantee that you'll notice the difference. God will direct your thoughts, plans, dreams, and actions for the rest of the day. You'll find yourself being a better steward of the minutes and hours. You'll discover greater sensitivity to God's presence and leading. Regardless of where you are right now in your life, you've been placed there by God. And God says, "I have a plan for you." There's comfort, hope, and assurance in His promise—trust Him!

> *Lord, I've been so scared to lose control in areas of my life that I've forgotten I was supposed to give You control. Take my thoughts, ideas, actions, and daily pursuits, Lord. I can't wait to walk in the assurance of Your plan.*

# Life Is Difficult

~•~

*A*nother year like this one, and I'm ready for that deserted island!" Life can be difficult, can't it? And God's process in your life may be painful at times or even confusing. There is a spiritual way to handle your struggles, and get ready, because it will go against your human nature: Treat trouble as an opportunity. I told you it'd be tricky! As difficult as it is to regard hard times as important to spiritual and personal growth, it is the change of perspective and heart that you need.

Your difficulty today is not just something to endure. Make adversity count for something positive by learning all you can from it. This doesn't mean that you have to downplay the hard times you or others face. Not at all. But let your trouble draw you closer to God and His leading in Your life. You will find the personal comfort, peace, and love of the living God.

*Lord, this trial has been wearing me down. Give me a new outlook as I face this trouble in Your strength and use it to walk more closely with You and to live with full dependence on Your grace.*

# The One Thing

~·~

*Y*ou likely have many pressing activities in your day. But are you making room for the one needed thing? Luke 10:40-43 reveals what that is: "Martha was distracted with much serving, and she approached Him and said, 'Lord, do You not care that my sister has left me to serve alone? Therefore tell her to help me.' And Jesus answered and said to her, 'Martha, Martha, you are worried and troubled about many things. But one thing is needed, and Mary has chosen that good part, which will not be taken away from her.'"

Think about your day. Make note of the way you spend your God-given time. A number of years ago, I was trying to find time for prayer and there just didn't seem to be any. Until I took a hard look at how much time was wasted running errands just to get out of the house. Taking breaks to watch TV. Chatting with friends. I actually had plenty of time. How about you? Can you make time to be with Jesus? It is the most important thing of all.

*Jesus, I am making room for the one needed thing! No more excuses. I want to sit at Your feet and spend time in fellowship, communion, and conversation with You, my sweet Lord.*

# Wise in Heart

~·~

*I*f I hear one more person telling me to manage my time better, I'm going to scream!" Well, I hate to be the one to make you holler right now, but believe me, your time, your life, and your priorities won't happen and won't line up with God's purpose for you without some management. But be encouraged—the rest of your life is ahead of you. And those minutes and hours, days and years are brimming with possibility. However, what you choose to do and what you choose not to do today impacts that future.

The mark of a woman who is wise in heart is that she enters all her tomorrows with great excitement and enthusiasm. And that doesn't happen without purpose, without taking time to plan ahead—one day at a time.

> *God, give me a heart of wisdom as I receive and use the gift of each day. The priorities I make today will affect how prepared I am to embrace Your purpose for me tomorrow. I don't want to miss a second of what You have planned for me.*

# Home Is Where the Heart Is

~•~

*M*arried or single, your home is an indicator of your maturity and a reflection of your care. What does the state of your home say about your life right now? The place that provides you with shelter, shared meals, and the comfort of God's provision is the heart of your and your family's life. And how you care for it sends a loud and clear message that leaves an impression on friends, neighbors, and anyone else who drops by.

Now, we all have "those days" when everything goes wrong and there's no time to clean the house. That's not what I'm talking about. I'm talking about the "usual." What does "usual" look like at your house? Treat the upkeep and atmosphere of your home sweet home with utmost care. It's not just what it says about you but what it says to those you love. The old saying, "Home is where the heart is" makes a lot of sense. Let your heart show and shine.

*Lord, give me a heart for my home so that it can reflect an attitude and desire to extend hospitality, peacefulness, and graciousness to everyone who enters. Help me, Lord. I really want the gift of my home to be a joy.*

# Wonderfully Made

~·~

You are wonderfully made! Have you let that truth sink in yet? Celebrate with the psalmist: "I will praise You, for I am fearfully and wonderfully made; marvelous are Your works, and that my soul knows very well" (Psalm 139:14). Rather than put down the way you look or resent your appearance, remember who you are in Christ.

This truth has been a lifesaver for me. It's eliminated all my concerns about self-image. My thinking goes like this: If God has transformed me from the inside out, caused me to become a new creation, and put His stamp of approval on my appearance, then who am I to find fault with His creation?

The Bible says you are wonderfully made! Take the next obvious step when you're looking in that mirror and thank God.

*God, I praise You for making me the way I am. It has taken me a long time to be able to appreciate who I am and how I am made. The more I express gratitude for my life, the more I can bring honor to You.*

# Be Thankful

~•~

*T*here is wise life-counsel in Colossians 3:15: "Let the peace of God rule in your hearts, to which also you were called in one body; and be thankful." *Be thankful.* Think on all you've been given in Christ. Let God's Word be a part of every area of your life, your heart, your goals, and your desires. Rejoice with psalms, hymns, and spiritual songs and let your gratitude shine. The more you develop your heart of gratitude, the more "generous" your spirit will become. You will have heart to give to others.

When your life is inspired by thankfulness, reach out to as many people as you can. Minister to as many people as you can in as many ways as you can. In the process you'll find yourself doing a lot of receiving. You'll find yourself quite blessed as you let God use you.

*Lord, I am so thankful for my life, my family, and for each new day. I want Your peace to fill and govern my heart, Lord. Show me how to breathe, walk, pray, share, sing, and live with gratitude.*

# Give Thanks

~•~

The more you think on gratitude, the more it will become a part of your spiritual perspective. The Bible says in Philippians 4:6, "Be anxious for nothing, but in everything by prayer and supplication, with thanksgiving, let your requests be made known to God." Prayer gives you some immunity against the world. When I make prayer a priority and seek God, a fire of passion for Him is ignited, fueled, and fanned. My time spent answering God's call to prayer causes me to point upward in gratitude and praise.

Here's an idea: Practice stopping in the middle of all your busyness and take time to pray. Give Him your anxieties, your concerns, and your deadlines. What does the hymn say? Turn your eyes on Jesus. And in *everything* give thanks!

*Father, release me from this anxiety. I give to You my needs, troubles, concerns, frets, and great joys. They are all a part of this life that I submit to You with thanksgiving. Use me for Your glory.*

# Stay Fit

~·~

Spiritual development is a lot like physical exercise. If you stop exercising, it might not show for a while. But one day you'll wake up to find every-
-thing sagging. And when you need your strength, it won't be there.

Don't let this be the way of your spiritual development. Don't deceive yourself by thinking that exercising your faith and investing in the discipline of spiritual growth doesn't matter. If you think you can get along just fine without the Bible or prayer, one day, you'll awaken to a big decision or a crisis, and you'll realize that you have very little spiritual strength to draw on.

Don't ignore your spiritual growth. You need to be in the Word of God to grow. Stay in it and stay fit!

*God, You are my workout partner. When I'm trained and strong in the ways of Your will, You help me work out and work through my struggles and my priorities. My time spent with You and in Your Word keeps me fit and faithful.*

# Thanks to God Who Leads Us

~·~

With the apostle Paul in 2 Corinthians 2:14 we can say, "Thanks be to God who always leads us in triumph in Christ." Have you felt those times of triumph and spiritual victory? I don't know about you, but I have peaks and valleys in my day. During the peaks, there's no stopping me. I'm running on all cylinders. Things are happening and moving along at a great pace. But during my valley times—watch out! I'm done, finished. And it may only be 2:00 in the afternoon. Sound familiar?

Diligence doesn't mean a frantic pace from morning until night. It means pursuing a fruitful pace of life from start to finish. Awaken in the morning with stewardship in mind for that one day. Follow the leading of Christ to purposefully move through the peaks and valleys. And give thanks to God at every step of the journey.

*Jesus, when I'm stumbling through the valleys and trying to find my footing, You are with me. And when I'm making my way to the top of a peak, You are there too. There isn't one part of my spiritual journey that is experienced apart from You. I'm so grateful.*

# Serious About Prayer

～•～

*G*od, give me the winning ticket!" If your prayer life has been directed toward the lottery or finding the perfect shoes, it's time to get serious about the practice and the intention of your prayers. The Bible says the effective, fervent prayer of a righteous woman, wife, mother, daughter, grandmother—whomever—avails much.

If it's true that prayer moves the hand of God, then we have work to do—serious work! So let's follow the examples and prayer patterns of some of the Bible's heroes of prayer and ask for the right things. Moses prayed to save a nation from death. Jonah prayed, and God delivered him from the stomach of a whale. Daniel prayed, and the angel locked the lions' jaws.

When you face your next challenge, you'll be glad that you've taken your conversation with God as seriously as He does.

*God, forgive me for silly or selfish prayers. I have so many sincere needs to lift up…like the people in my life who I pray will come to know You. And the past hurts in my family that need healing. Thank You for hearing the prayers of my heart.*

# Thanks in All Circumstances

~·~

First Thessalonians 5:18 says, "Give thanks in all circumstances." And it tells you why: "For this is God's will for you in Christ Jesus" (NIV). Giving thanks in the good, the bad, and the uncomfortable situations can be a tough assignment, but with God's help, it can be done. You can face life with joy and in the power and grace of the Holy Spirit. God is still in control. He is still sovereign. He is still all-powerful. He is still able. And He always will be.

Pay attention and look for the good that is coming from your trial. In the darkness of what's taking place, you may have to search for it. But Psalm 103:2 says, "Bless the Lord, O my soul, and forget not all His benefits." Don't let even one of God's blessings go unnoticed. Write them down. God is good and worthy of praise.

*Father, today I want to give You praise and thanks. Every circumstance brings me to You because You are the Author of my life. You are Creator, King, and Savior. I am blessed as Your daughter.*

# *Be* Content

~·~

*D*iscontentment can sneak up on you. The most common underlying cause of arguments between a wife and a husband is a financial matter or a difference of opinion about money. If you've felt this tension in your marriage, there is something you can do—invest in contentment. It helps if you're content in your heart.

Contentment enables you to look at something and say, "I can live with it or without it and still be at peace." Satisfaction, identity, and contentment sought and found in the love of the Lord offers freedom and security far more valuable than any new house or investment portfolio.

This attitude will also provide you and your husband with a calm, common ground of purpose for those times when you do need to talk about money matters. You married for richer or poorer. Choose to be rich in contentment!

*Lord, I can feel the tension leave my body when I think of You being in control of my life and my future. I truly am content with the blessings You provide. Keep me from letting my wants take over the true spiritual needs of my life and my marriage.*

# Be Willful

~·~

*H*ave your thoughts ever drifted during a sermon or while someone is praying? Godly thinking isn't easy. It takes focus, effort, and an attentive mind and heart. You can develop your spiritual agility.

Make a decision each day to concentrate on the Lord. Think about verses you read in the Bible. Think about God's character and love. These are willful choices you make. The Bible says, "Whatever things are true, whatever things are noble, whatever things are just, whatever things are pure, whatever things are lovely, whatever things are of good report, if there is any virtue and if there is anything praiseworthy—meditate on these things" (Philippians 4:8). Think on these things, and it will be life-changing. Take time each day to praise God. Use the psalms in the Bible. Psalm 119:164 says, "Seven times a day I praise You." Try it! Make it a habit throughout your day to praise the Lord.

*God, I want to be willful in my pursuit of godly character. Give me a mind and heart that are so intertwined with Your presence and Word that my first thoughts are of You and my first steps are always in Your direction.*

# Frazzle-free

*L*ife can be frustrating. But when frustration and anger become everyday events at your house, it's time to do some soul searching. You can provide a true haven for your family when there's no screaming, no fits, no meltdowns, no lashing out, no blaming, and no slamming. A perfect home? No, that's not the goal. But do all you can to be a woman who is serious about giving your life and home to God's control. Do this when things are going wonderfully and do this when you feel frazzled.

Every day is the day to give over to God's hope for your family. Oh, to be able to walk through each trial with balance, calmness, with a sober mind, and with a frazzle-free head and heart! This is what God desires of you and for you.

*Lord, I want to exchange the chaos for Your control. The craziness for Your calm. The pandemonium for Your peace. And the unruliness for Your sovereign rule. Be the Lord of my heart and home.*

# Don't Be Slanderous

~·~

You can't be loving while you are cutting someone down with your words. Unfortunately, this bad habit comes all too naturally to a lot of people. The Bible says emphatically—don't be slanderous in your speech. You can start protecting yourself from this ungodly behavior by avoiding people who talk about others in a malicious way.

It's too easy to get caught up in the moment. Never forget that it's Satan who's at the source of evil speaking. Stay busy. Choose carefully who you hang out with. Don't mention names or tell stories about other people. Pray for yourself in this area and God will help guard your heart, mind, and tongue from unkind words. Protect yourself and your reputation. Firmly deal with gossip as the sin it is. Confess it. Dear friend, use your mouth to glorify God.

*God, I've let gossip creep back into my conversations. Forgive me for being loose with my words and casual with the way I talk about people. I want my speech to be godly and edifying so it encourages others and honors You.*

# Life Essentials

~·~

*H*ow about some exercise? No, not that kind, though that is good too. I'm thinking of a regimen as something a little different. I call this exercise routine my "life essentials." It's a way to exercise discipline as you pursue the goal of living as a godly woman—a woman who's in control of self instead of controlled *by* self. A woman who lives a steady lifestyle of self-restraint. A woman characterized by keeping appetites, actions, and passions moderate in their intensity. A woman who displays mental and emotional balance.

Come up with your own definition of moderation, of self-control, based on God's Word. It'll help you control those appetites for ungodly actions so you can put your energy and effort toward godly behavior.

*God, help me contain my appetites. Give me strength today. And remind me that "more is better" only when it relates to more of You, Your Word, and Your control in my life.*

# Check Your Priorities

~·~

*T*here's no way I'd ever consider dumping my career—David's not giving up his!" Let's talk, shall we? Everything you do is to be done excellently. And that's going to require that you constantly check your priorities. Reviewing them first thing every morning will help you keep your marriage, family, home, and job in perspective.

Whether you are married or single, your home is more important in God's big picture than your job. The time spent with your husband and children is your greatest and grandest work for the day. And if you are a single parent, you know how precious time with your kids is. My urging is this: Whatever decisions you do make, don't view your job as more important than the work you do at home! Set priorities for how you spend time, money, and activities so that the family comes first.

*Father, help me decide what is best for my family and my home life. I'm overcommitted and growing tired of always being tired. Give me a clear vision for ways I can put my family first. I pray to lean into Your strength and trust Your provision more than ever.*

# The Highest Calling

~•~

*Y*ou have a calling. Did you realize that? God's first and highest calling on your life is to Himself. Seek to draw close to Him in all ways and seek His transforming love. What's in your heart affects your behavior. God asks that your actions represent your relationship with Him.

The Bible says to "be reverent in behavior" (Titus 2:3). Even though that verse is addressed to older women, it wraps its arms around every woman of every age and circumstance. Why? Because it calls all of us to be holy and godly. "There is one body and one Spirit, just as you were called in one hope of your calling; one Lord, one faith, one baptism; one God and Father of all, who is above all, and through all, and in you all" (Ephesians 4:4-6).

What a gift it is to be a woman who walks with God every day of her life! There is no greater calling.

*Lord, Your calling and love bring worth and wonder to my life. My daily pursuit of Your heart and Your Word leads me to serve this high calling. May all that I do and all that I become reflect my relationship with You.*

# Favorite Scriptures

# Books by Elizabeth George

- Beautiful in God's Eyes
- Breaking the Worry Habit…Forever
- Finding God's Path Through Your Trials
- Following God with All Your Heart
- Life Management for Busy Women
- Loving God with All Your Mind
- A Mom After God's Own Heart
- Quiet Confidence for a Woman's Heart
- Raising a Daughter After God's Own Heart
- The Remarkable Women of the Bible
- Small Changes for a Better Life
- Walking with the Women of the Bible
- A Wife After God's Own Heart
- A Woman After God's Own Heart*
- A Woman After God's Own Heart*
  Deluxe Edition
- A Woman After God's Own Heart*—
  A Daily Devotional
- A Woman After God's Own Heart* Collection
- A Woman After God's Own Heart
  DVD and Workbook
- A Woman's Call to Prayer
- A Woman's Daily Walk with God
- A Woman's Guide to Making Right Choices
- A Woman's High Calling
- A Woman's Walk with God
- A Woman Who Reflects the Heart of Jesus
- A Young Woman After God's Own Heart
- A Young Woman After God's Own Heart—
  A Devotional
- A Young Woman's Call to Prayer
- A Young Woman's Guide to Making
  Right Choices
- A Young Woman's Walk with God

## Study Guides

- Beautiful in God's Eyes
  Growth & Study Guide
- Finding God's Path Through Your Trials
  Growth & Study Guide
- Following God with All Your Heart
  Growth & Study Guide
- Life Management for Busy Women
  Growth & Study Guide
- Loving God with All Your Mind
  Growth & Study Guide
- A Mom After God's Own Heart
  Growth & Study Guide
- The Remarkable Women of the Bible
  Growth & Study Guide
- Small Changes for a Better Life
  Growth & Study Guide
- A Wife After God's Own Heart
  Growth & Study Guide
- A Woman After God's Own Heart*
  Growth & Study Guide
- A Woman's Call to Prayer
  Growth & Study Guide
- A Woman's High Calling
  Growth & Study Guide
- A Woman's Walk with God
  Growth & Study Guide
- A Woman Who Reflects the Heart of Jesus
  Growth & Study Guide

## Children's Books

- A Girl After God's Own Heart
- God's Wisdom for Little Girls
- A Little Girl After God's Own Heart

# Books by Jim George

- 10 Minutes to Knowing the Men and
  Women of the Bible
- The Bare Bones Bible* Facts
- The Bare Bones Bible* Handbook
- The Bare Bones Bible* Handbook for Teens
- A Husband After God's Own Heart
- A Leader After God's Own Heart
- A Man After God's Own Heart
- The Man Who Makes a Difference
- The Remarkable Prayers of the Bible
- A Young Man After God's Own Heart
- A Young Man's Guide to Making Right Choices

# Books by Jim & Elizabeth George

- God Loves His Precious Children
- God's Wisdom for Little Boys
- A Little Boy After God's Own Heart

## About the Author

**Elizabeth George** is a bestselling author whose passion is to teach the Bible in a way that changes women's lives. She has more than 7 million books in print, including *A Woman After God's Own Heart* and *A Woman's Daily Walk with God*.

Elizabeth, her books, her ministry, and to sign up to receive her daily devotions, and to join her on Facebook and Twitter, visit her website at:

www.ElizabethGeorge.com